The Breakup Workbook 3.0

Commonsense Breakup Advice for Everyone

FIRST EDITION

M.J. Acharya

Copyright

© 2024 BHG Books

All rights reserved. No part of this publication may be reproduced, distributed, or transmitted in any form or by any means, including photocopying, recording, or other electronic or mechanical methods, without the prior written permission of the publisher, except in the case of brief quotations embodied in critical reviews and certain other noncommercial uses permitted by copyright law. For permission requests, write to the publisher, addressed "Attention: Permissions Coordinator," at breakupworkbook@gmail.com

Although every precaution has been taken to verify the accuracy of the information contained herein, the author and publisher assume no responsibility for any errors or omissions. No liability is assumed for damages that may result from the use of information contained within.

Publisher: BHG Books

Publisher's Cataloging-in-Publication data: Acharya, M.J./The Breakup Workbook 3.0/ M.J. Acharya p. cm.

ISBN: 978-0-9908232-5-4

First Edition.

Terms

The contents listed here are for informational purposes only. Nothing contained in this book is or should be considered or used as a substitute for professional medical or mental health advice, diagnosis, or treatment.

Never disregard medical advice from your doctor or other qualified health care providers or delay seeking it because of something you have read in this book or on our website. We urge you to seek the advice of your physician or other qualified health professionals with any questions you may have regarding a medical or mental health condition. In case of emergency, please call your doctor or 911 immediately.

The information contained on or provided through The Breakup Workbook 3.0 is provided on an "as is" basis, without any warranty, express or implied. Everything you read and apply through this book is voluntary and at your own risk.

The author does not recommend or endorse any products, services, tests, opinions, or information that may be provided by any sites mentioned within The Breakup Workbook 3.0 and accepts no responsibility for any content or material provided within those sites.

CONTENTS

INTRODUCTION. 5

THE BREAKUP WORKBOOK 3.0 9

01. Forgive Yourself. 12

02. Set Boundaries. 16

03. Throw a Pity Party. 28

04. Sex—To Have Or Not To Have? 34

05. Set Small Daily Goals. 38

06. "The Breakup Diet.". 41

07. Write Down The Things You Loved... 50

08. Question Your Relationship. 54

09. Make Your Place Your Own Again. 72

10. Writing to Heal.. 84

11. Get In Touch With Your Spiritual Side.. 86

12. Self-Soothe To Heal. 90

13. Write A Letter To Your Ex (But Don't Send It!). 95

14. Sing 97

15. Visit The Past. 100

16. Use Anger As A Crutch. 103

17. Exercise To Heal. 108

18. Analyze It. 112

19. Speak with a Therapist. 116

20. Phone-A-Friend. 119

21. Begin to Repair Your Self-Esteem. 122

22. Dispose of Your Ex's Stuff. 127

23. Meet with Your Ex. 129

24. Write The Future As It Really Would Have Been. 133

25. Envision Your New Future. 137

26. Write Your Own "Happily Ever After." 141

27. Create Personal Goals. 145

28. Choose the Right People to Date. 149

29. Make a Dating Game Plan 155

30. Get Out of The House if You Haven't Yet! 162

31. FINAL THOUGHTS. 169

RESOURCES. 172

INTRODUCTION

I can't believe it! This book has been around for 20 years now. It was the first workbook of its kind to come out on the market—way back in 2004—when I owned the website BrokenHeartedGirl.com. I was a bit ahead of the times then, asking people to write in their books (the horror!), but if you look around now, you'll see A LOT of competition for breakup workbooks you can write in. Like a lot, a lot! So, I'm so glad and grateful you've found the original "The Breakup Workbook"—so just know you're in good hands.

What you'll find in this book:

- A commonsense game plan for helping you get over your ex; supported by advice from therapists, psychologists, and other mental health professionals.

- Intuitive writing exercises (lots of them) to help you figure out your feelings.

- Suggestions on how to find a therapist, whom to call when you're depressed & what to do when depression gets out of control.

- Suggestions on healthy ways to eat while you're getting over your ex.

- What to do if you have children and you're going through a breakup.

- What to do if you still live with your ex.

- Ideas about ways to start or keep up with an exercise regimen while you're getting over the relationship.

- Tools to help with low self-esteem and rebuilding self-confidence.

- Things to do while you're getting over the ex (instead of staring at the wall, drinking too much and eating the contents of your entire refrigerator).

- Ways to take back your space and make your home your own again.

At the end of this book, you should:

- Be able to see your relationship from a new perspective.

- Understand that the relationship ended for reasons beyond your control, accept it and begin to move forward.

- Be armed with tools to make good decisions about the next person you date.

- Be able to recognize red flags so you know when to leave & know how to recognize an unhealthy person/pattern before you get too involved.
- Be able to envision a happy, healthy future without your ex.

There's no magical advice in this book that will suddenly jolt you into healing.

It takes time to get over someone. Our hope is that one or all the exercises in the book will resonate with you, help you see your relationship from a new perspective, and help you emerge from this breakup a happier, healthier, you—ready to take on the world!

It's all about you:

This book is all about you. All these exercises ask you to write about your specific relationship and think about how it affected you. Use this book as your own breakup diary and customize it to fit your specific breakup situation. If an exercise doesn't fit or work within your circumstances, feel free to SKIP IT (just don't skip them all, because that isn't going to help anybody!).

There is a private Facebook group for people looking for advice on their situation: www.facebook.com/groups/breakupworkbook3/. I encourage you to respond to posts from others. It's where you can go to post about your issue and get feedback from other people in the same situation. It's also where you can spend time helping someone else get through their breakup—because believe it or not—you do have good advice to give. Sometimes it's just harder to take your own advice and it's easier to get it from someone else.

So, take a deep breath, get out your pen, and get ready to do some hard work. I promise that time heals all wounds. It's what you do in that time that makes you emerge from your breakup "better" or "bitter." Aim for better!

THE BREAKUP WORKBOOK 3.0

Getting dumped by someone you really loved sucks! Yesterday, you were happy and, in a relationship—and today, you don't even know if you can get out of bed. You thought that you were with THE ONE. Now you are left alone with only nagging questions to keep you company in the night: How could this happen to you? How are you going to get through it? How will you ever move on?

Let's be clear: there's no magical solution to heartache. Ask anyone and they'll tell you that it takes time to get over a breakup. Like everything in life, getting over someone is a process. You've probably heard that it's like the grieving process—and it is. Get ready because you're going to experience a battery of emotions: remorse, denial, anger, depression, hysteria, and at times you may even believe that you're going crazy. But to put it in perspective, getting dumped certainly isn't as bad as if someone you love really passes away. Right?

You'll likely go from staring into space and bursting into tears, to screaming at the top of your lungs, throwing things across the room, and reminiscing about the past. But invariably, all these emotions are going to help you heal. So, no matter how silly or embarrassed you may feel, don't push these fits of rage or crying away. Embrace these feelings! Do the amount of screaming, crying, and yelling that is right for you. You'll know when the appropriate amount has been done because you'll begin to feel better. It could take weeks, or even months, but **you will** begin to feel better.

We (the therapists quoted in this book, and me) will help you stay focused on recovery while you go through every emotion—from sadness and despair to eventual happiness. Staying the course and know that completing the exercises in this book could stop you from making phone calls to your ex at all hours, Instagram-stalking your ex, reading all their Tweets (X), texting incessantly (and inappropriately), swearing to get revenge, plotting to run into your ex somewhere, or doing something harmful to yourself or others.

We invite you to work through all the exercises completely—even overdo them. We want you to thoughtfully complete each exercise in order. You may be tempted to complete the entire book in one night, but we strongly suggest you take your time getting through it—otherwise the book won't help. As we said, it takes time to get over a breakup. Take the time to focus on the exercises in this book.

Take comfort in the knowledge that you will get over your ex. But until then, do the work necessary to find yourself again, so that when you're done healing you can take everything that's wonderful about you and put it into a new relationship. Let's get started.

EXERCISE 1:

FORGIVE YOURSELF.

The decision to buy a breakup book is not a light one. Chances are you've either gone through a breakup that has left you traumatized, or you've done something you feel badly about. And whether it's not showing up to work, not being able to summon the energy to get out of bed to get to an appointment on time, crying too much, texting your ex too much, emailing too much, calling too much, stalking your ex on social media, or showing up unannounced to your ex's house, you've recognized that the breakup is hurting you, and more importantly, you've recognized that you could use some help getting over it.

Believe it or not, recognizing unhealthy behavior is actually a healthy first step toward moving forward. In fact, Marina Williams, a licensed mental health counselor out of Boston, MA, says, "The first step towards change is recognizing what hasn't been working for you.

It can be painful and embarrassing to admit that past attitudes and behaviors were self-destructive, but it is ultimately a healing process. When we do this, we come out of break-ups as stronger people and better future partners. We recognize the unhealthy behavior, make a promise to ourselves never to do it again, and then find a healthy new behavior to take its place. That is the 'gift' we receive with every failed relationship. That is how we achieve personal growth."

In fact, a lot of the thingsss you've done or may be thinking of doing may merely be a direct result of anxiety (meaning, you're not crazy!). Answer this question: "Do you find yourself thinking about your ex more now that you are broken up than when you were together?"

If so, Williams says, "Thinking about your ex a lot is going to produce a great deal of anxiety. You're going to naturally feel very motivated to try to alleviate that anxiety. Unfortunately, people often think that the way to alleviate their anxiety is to try to get in contact with their ex (such as through repeatedly calling, texting, or emailing them). Another way to do this is by setting up "chance encounters" by frequenting places you know your ex visits often."

This can backfire on you—and may have already backfired on you. As Williams says, "Unfortunately, what happens is that oftentimes when you do get in contact with the ex, it doesn't go well. Your ex may react with hostility, indifference, or worse, give mixed messages. This just results in more anxiety and more attempts to get in contact with the ex to alleviate that anxiety. A vicious cycle can result, one that can lead to an escalation of 'stalking behavior'."

So, maybe you feel that you're not getting over your ex quickly enough. Maybe you think that all the feelings you have are not normal. Maybe you did something of which you're ashamed. Whatever led you to this point, please just stop everything you're doing and do one thing: forgive yourself. You're allowed to go slightly off the rails when your world is turned upside down. It's perfectly normal to feel out of balance and <u>you're not crazy</u>. So, if you haven't done so already, forgive your missteps so you can move forward.

If you do feel as if your anxiety has gotten the best of you, or you feel that your behavior may be illegal (stalking, keying cars, writing threatening emails), then we urge you to flip to the "Resources" section at the back of this book to consult a mental health professional. You can continue with this book while consulting a therapist or psychiatrist. All we care about here is that you're healthy, even if you're not currently happy.

In this book, you're going to start doing the work to stop this sort of behavior. You're going to learn how to curb your anxiety, accept your feelings and allow yourself to let go of your ex. It will take some time, but just know that recognizing that you need help to get through this breakup is a healthy first step in your recovery process.

So, stop everything you're doing, and say these words out loud, "I forgive myself."

You're already on your way toward getting over this breakup.

EXERCISE 2:
SET BOUNDARIES.

A lot of breakup books stress that you should immediately and completely have no contact with your ex while you endeavor to recover from the breakup. And we, too, subscribe to that theory—with a caveat. We advise you to avoid your ex for at least the first two weeks after the breakup. Just think about it as putting yourself in a protective "healing cocoon" so you have time to breathe and put your relationship into perspective. Your ex may reach out to you, but now it's important to set your boundaries and let them know you need space.

After you've been successful for a week or two, you might want to speak with your ex for the sole purpose of seeking closure (and only then if you want to and think it would be beneficial). After that, you can continue your journey to recovery.

If you have children, or live with your ex, please keep reading this chapter for advice on those situations.

You may be thinking: "Well, we said that we're going to be friends. I shouldn't avoid my ex. This, therefore, doesn't apply to me."

Maybe that's true, but the healthy thing to do is give yourself time to heal.

Ask yourself these questions and be honest:

- Do you only want to be friends because you dream of getting back together?
- Do you only want to be friends because you want to sleep with your ex again and hope that by doing so, you'll get back together?
- Do you only want to be friends because you wish to insert yourself into their life as a trusted sounding board—listening to the gory and intimate details about your ex's dating life—just so you can help influence/manipulate their decisions?
- Do you only want to be friends because you're secretly plotting your revenge?

Maybe, or maybe not, right?

You may also believe that avoidance is crazy or just plain cruel. Fine. Be friends months from now if keeping your ex in your life is that important to you. But if your sanity is equally important, we advise you to hold off for a short while. If you're asked why you've fallen off the face of the earth, just tell the truth before you cut off contact. If your ex really wants to be friends, they will have to practice some understanding and patience.

It's not unreasonable to ask for space. If your ex gets angry with you over your need for time to yourself, then we suggest you question their intention for asking you to be friends. Friends respect one another. Hopefully your old flame will respect your right to grieve.

This is where a favorite quote comes into play: "Having the love of your life leave you and say, 'we can still be friends' is like your dog dying and your mom saying, 'you can still keep it'."

So, let's focus on you. That's why you got this book in the first place, right? Here are some basic avoidance tactics:

Establish your support network. First thing in the morning, call or email a few friends or family members who will support you—even if you're a crying, blubbery, neurotic mess. Let's face it: some friends are like siblings while others are just "bar friends." Pick the ones who are closest to you and ask them for their help.

Don't be proud. They are your friends and we're sure they will be more than willing to have your back.

Now tell them the plan: they are going to play defense against your offense 24 hours a day 7 days a week, for at least two weeks straight. When you're itching to call the ex, you'll call all of them instead. When you're dying to fire off a text, you'll text them instead. Their job is to simply respond to you and talk you out of it.

Join a cyber support network. When you sense you're testing the limits of your friends' good natures, log on to our private page at www.facebook.com/groups/breakupworkbook3/ and speak with other people who are also going through this no-contact phase. It may help to speak with someone going through the same anguish. It'll help even more to speak with others who are working through the same book. You already have something in common. We've broken the ice for you.

Do whatever you have to do. A support network alone isn't going to save you from your anxiety. A lot of people feel like they are going crazy when experiencing "ex-withdrawal." To some extent, everyone goes a little mad during this stage. Here are some tricks to help you get through the day:

Step away from the computer. When you're at your wits' end and feel like you absolutely, positively must send that email or DM—even after everyone in your support network has tried to talk you out of it, take a walk. Like they say in the movies, "Step away from the gun!" At work? Just get up and leave your desk. You can head to the water cooler and listen to some office gossip (always fun), or step outside and get some fresh air. At home? Go take a walk outside, jump on your Peloton, or play with your pet.

Ditch the cell phone. When you're at home and want to call, go for a drive with your cell phone in your glove compartment. Go see a movie since you're obligated to turn off your cell phone. Go to a friend's house and leave your cell phone in the car. Sleep over at a friends' place and give your cell phone to them to hide…Just do whatever it is that you must do to avoid calling or texting the ex. And if the temptation is too much, then, guess what? There's an app for that! Check out the App store on your phone and pick the one that's right for you. Here are a few:

- Drunk Mode Keyboard
- Drunk Dial. No!
- No Contact Rule

Write down the worst thing your ex ever said to you and post it where you'll see it daily. Every time you get an urge to make contact, read that piece of paper. It will hurt to read it, but those nasty words will help you realize what a jerk your ex can be—ultimately leading to the realization that your ex is not perfect. And maybe they didn't say anything nasty. But said, "I'm not ready to get married", or "I don't want to be with you any longer," or "It's not you, it's me." Whatever it was that was said that hurt you, write it down. Remember why the breakup happened.

Don't answer your ex's phone calls (unless you must because you share children —more on that soon). Maybe your ex is trying to ensure your friendship won't suffer. Maybe your ex is just trying to sleep with you. Maybe they're love-bombing you. Maybe they want to get back together. Whatever the reason for the call, don't answer the phone. Let it go to voicemail and after you listen to what they have to say, then you can decide whether to return the call. We suggest that unless your ex apologizes and asks for reconciliation, you should just wait. Chances are you'll call back anyway and end up back at square one. But that's okay. It's hard to ignore someone when they are reaching out to you. Our point is, just be aware of the true intentions and try not to place too much importance on the call.

Stay away from your ex's hangouts. Perhaps they may have been your hangouts together, but right now that's all semantics. Avoid the bars, restaurants, the grocery stores, dog runs, and jogging trails frequented by your ex. You don't need to do this forever. Just for now. If you must drive an extra five minutes to go to another grocery store, then do it. This is all for your mental health, so go the extra mile or two in these scenarios.

Go to lunch with someone else. If you and your ex used to go to lunch together every day or on the weekends, start a new tradition. Maybe for the first few days, or weeks, you'll choose to cry at your desk during your lunch hour, or on the weekends in the safety of your own home. But eventually, you'll get the strength up to actually eat. Call your friends and/or coworkers and institute a new lunch routine—one that doesn't involve your ex.

If you work with your ex: avoidance may seem hard, if not downright impossible. Simple advice is necessary in this situation:

- **Take time off** if you can do it without jeopardizing your job.

- **Show up to work extra early**, so you don't see the ex in the parking lot.

- **Change your lunch schedule**, so you can avoid the ex at the cafeteria.

- **Don't give in to the company gossip**. Don't tell people what happened. When they ask, just tell them that you're "okay." Don't say anything positive or negative. That way, when it's time to seek closure, your ex will be likely to agree to a meeting.

- **Be strictly professional** if you have to email or call the ex for work reasons. The last thing you want is to get written up for calling your ex mean names on company email.

- **Lean on your support network.** It's what they're there for!

What if I live with my ex?

Psychotherapist Cynthia C. McKay, J.D., M.A. gives this advice for those couples who are still living together while trying to heal from a breakup, "One of the most difficult maneuvers in a relationship is the decision to separate. The situation becomes particularly toxic and complicated by the inability of one party to actually depart. This might be due to extenuating circumstances such as an unbreakable lease, an unsellable house, or the inability to find affordable housing."

But you can manage the situation. McKay says, "In order to make a bad situation tolerable, write up an agreement. You are no longer a couple, yet you'll need to find neutral ways in which to remain under the same roof. Each individual should have a pad and pen and make a list. Include your terms succinctly and then negotiate any unclear areas that could be cause for confusion in the future."

Here are some guidelines:

- **Be civilized.** Understand that you both know so much about each other, that the idea of pushing one's buttons will be easier for you both. Face the fact that familiarity can indeed breed contempt, so take a breath before using any "old ammunition" in order to make a point.

- **Respect boundaries.** You can no longer abide by the "open door policy" you previously had. Respect a closed door, an occupied bath area and refrain from making yourself at home with your "roommate's" gourmet cookies, imported Jamaican Blue Coffee or the freshly baked Pasta primavera.

- **Take responsibility for yourself.** Do your own cleanup, your own laundry and divide the bills and other expenses amicably.

- **Put a time limit on the uncoupling.** Have a plan in place to move, reserve an apartment or find another roommate within the time limit agreed upon.

- **Play fairly.** Do not bring dates home, particularly for an overnight hookup. It's just undignified and will certainly cause hurt feelings. If you do feel the need to parade around a new guy or gal, imagine how awkward the explanation will sound as you try to explain why you still reside with your ex.

- **Don't drink and reminisce**. If you think it's "probably okay" for you and your ex to lounge on the couch, have a few drinks and visit the "good times"- DON'T. It didn't work before, and you need to go on about your life. Because the situation arises and it's convenient, pass on any temptation that will inevitably prolong your misery.

- **Be kind.** It's over, you may be hurt, anxious and mad but don't punish your ex by refusing to make proper arrangements for pets or even kids you had together. When you're dividing up the possessions, if you refuse to include the matching saucers with the coffee cups, you're just being mean.

- **Avoid punitive behavior.** In a breakup, there usually is one major factor responsible for the uncoupling. An affair, lying or just basic incompatibility. While you're under the same roof, avoid insults; don't throw the past up in the face of your ex. Let it go.

- **Move on**. The breakup has been made, and the physical separation is imminent. Plan on how you'll take care of yourself both physically and mentally so you can leave the past in the past and begin again.

What if I share children with my ex?

Mental health counselor Marina Williams says, "Having firm rules and boundaries about visitation will be helpful for everyone." Here are her tips for those who share children with an ex:

- **Keep communication 'strictly business.'** An arrangement or schedule can be drawn up in order to develop a routine where little communication is needed.

- **Let someone else schedule the arrangements.** For example, if your child is a teenager, they may be able to take over the scheduling rather than relying on you as the go-between.

- **Think of alternate possibilities,** like dropping off your child with a neutral third-party, such as a grandparent, and then have your ex pick up your child from there.

Final Thoughts:

When you're in the throes of anxiety, sometimes you just need help getting through the rough patches. We understand how hard it can be to act sane 100% of the time when you're going through a breakup. So again, do whatever it is that you must do, just don't call or text or email or DM or tweet or Instagram, or contact your ex in any way, shape, or form for now. Cut yourself off cold turkey for just a little while. Remember that you're in a healing cocoon and try to allow yourself that time to heal.

As a reminder, you will be able to get in touch eventually, just not right away, and certainly not while you're so vulnerable. Just keep working through the exercises in this book and you'll get there in time.

EXERCISE 3:
THROW A PITY PARTY.

We know what other books tell you. The cool thing to do is to act like you don't care about your ex, ignore all your feelings, and just move on. However, the healthy thing to do is to acknowledge your hurt feelings, accept them, embrace them, and ultimately let them go. So, screw it, let's have a pity party!

So, what exactly is a pity party? Glad you asked…According to a post on Urban Dictionary, a pity party is: "A way of experiencing grief, in which you spend your time feeling sorry for yourself and whining endlessly about how crappy your life is."

So why should you have one? That's easy! To experience the full, unadulterated, horrible feelings surrounding the abrupt end of your relationship! In other words, allow yourself to feel exactly how you felt the minute you were dumped. Recognize your grief and embrace it. Then unleash it appropriately.

So how do you have a pity party? Good question. Here are some ideas:

- **Close all the curtains in your home to give yourself some privacy**.

- **Review all the liquor bottles and/or beer from your cabinet and mix some drinks** (if you're of age, of course!). If you drink, don't drive

- **Cry.** Every so often you can dramatically scream out, "Why me?" while shaking your fist in the air.

- **Find every card your ex ever gave you and read them all out loud.** If your ex has never given you a card, then curse them for never thinking that far ahead.

- **Order take out.** In fact, order the most fatty, tasty thing you can think of and eat it all without guilt.

- **When you're done eating your takeout, grab a pint of ice cream** or a bake a cake and just enjoy it.

- **Read every text message from your ex** in your phone. Bonus points for reading them aloud in a sarcastic voice.

- **Read every single email or DM you ever exchanged.** If you're feeling ambitious, print them out and then shred the messages one by one.

- **Listen to every sad song on your iTunes** and sing them out loud - even if your voice is horrible.

- **Review all of the gchat conversations** you two have ever had.

- **Watch sappy movies where people do crazy stuff that never happens in real life** (like stopping a plane on the runway).

- **Throw your pillows against the wall to release physical tension** (be careful not to break anything).

- **Take out a piece of paper and write down the future you had imagined with your ex;** the wedding, the kids, the house you had imagined you'd live in, how you'd grow old together…all of it. Then tear up the paper.

- **Once again, cry.** Feel the pain and let out your grief. This is your pity party, and nobody has to know about it but you!

Pity Party Part 2 (the healthier version):

After you've had your completely guilt-free pity party, we suggest this exercise from psychotherapist Rachel

Weinstein, MA, LCPC (www.rachelweinsteintherapy.com).

Weinstein says, "There are a lot of great exercises and ideas in this book about how to get through to the other side of painful feelings. This exercise is kind of the flip side of all of that. A main purpose of Buddhist meditation is to get close and comfy with pain or discomfort to in an effort to cut down on the struggle most of us go through in order to get away from pain. It's based on the idea that a lot of extra suffering we experience in our lives comes from resisting pain and clinging to pleasure."

Weinstein continues, "So here you are going through a very painful experience. Although there are lots of things you can do proactively to heal, you can also find some peace in gently accepting the loss and grief with which you find yourself, knowing that it (like everything else) is impermanent."

So, here's how you do it:

- Sit comfortably in an upright position cross-legged on the floor, or on a chair or couch.

- Close your eyes and bring your attention to your breath. When your mind wanders, gently notice it, and bring your attention back to your breath. Do this for a couple of minutes.

- Next, bring your attention to the sadness (or anger, frustration, etc.) that you feel. Notice what it feels like. Notice where it exists in your body. Is it hot? Is it tight?

- Now, as you breathe in, imagine breathing in the pain or sadness. As you breathe out, imagine breathing out cooling and healing to your pain. This is both simple and very complex at the same time.

But you don't have to only do this exercise now when you're in pain. In the future, you can do it for others, and it can also help you in the long run. As Weinstein says, "You can perform this exercise for your own pain, and you can also do it for others in pain. You can connect with the pain in the world and use it to help open your heart to compassion. As Pema Chodron, an American Buddhist nun says, 'Use what seems like poison as medicine. Use your personal suffering as the path to compassion for all beings.'"

So, whether you just sit on the couch and cry, or connect with your pain using Weinstein's exercise (or do both), we hope you to take time to recognize the fact that you're in pain and we hope that you're not ashamed to allow yourself to feel that pain. Emoting is good, especially when you're in a safe, comfortable, appropriate environment.

While you're emoting, you shouldn't do anything extreme like delete your ex from social media, make a detailed announcement on any social platform, or change your relationship status, or do anything that's going to cause an outpouring of emotion from other people. Right now, just experience your own emotions without regard to anyone else. You can worry about all that kind of stuff tomorrow or the next day. Just take some time to grieve.

Keep in mind that there is no pity party timeframe. Some people have a pity party for hours and some will have one for days. Just allow yourself to cry until you can't cry anymore. Don't try to be strong or ignore the pain. We know so many people who skip this stage and end up suppressing their emotions, only to unleash them at the most inappropriate times. The last thing you want to do is break down during an important business meeting or presentation. Just allow yourself to experience your pain so you can let it go.

And when you're finished with your pity party and fully ready to begin letting go of this pain, begin the next exercise. But do take your time to feel, embrace and eventually release your emotions. It's an important part of the healing process. Just remember that getting over someone you truly cared for is a marathon and not a sprint.

EXERCISE 4:

SEX—TO HAVE OR NOT TO HAVE?

This isn't really an exercise, but it is good advice to follow while you're getting over your traumatic breakup. I wanted to bring it up early in the book because it's important to your recovery. A lot of people say, "the best way to get over someone is to get under someone else." And maybe that's a good distraction, but when you're getting over a breakup that has hurt you this badly, you may want to heed the following advice:

Relationship therapist Nina Batista, LCSW, CNAST, CCT www.ninabatistacounseling.com says this about hooking up immediately after a breakup: "Wanting to immediately hookup after a breakup is a form of avoidance and seeking of external validation. A breakup is a loss—it requires a grieving process. Many people immediately hookup with someone else to numb themselves of the feelings of grief—as sex releases chemicals in our brain that make us feel happy and connected. The problem with this is that you're not addressing the underlying grief, and you may end up prematurely entering a relationship due to your unresolved grief. It's like getting drunk instead of dealing with your emotions (you're putting a band aid on a bullet wound)—so the wound is not going to heal, it's going to get infected and cause issues in your life in other ways".

"It is imperative for you to properly grieve your breakup—reflect on what worked and didn't work in the relationship, and how you can improve."

Steffo Shambo, founder of the Tantric Academy (https://tantricacademy.com/) advises, "Having rebound sex immediately after a breakup rarely leads to emotional healing. It's best to process the loss first before pursuing new partners. Prioritize emotional healing before physical needs. However, consenting casual sex between adults is not inherently unhealthy if both parties understand it's temporary."

So, there's some good advice about having sex too early, but what about masturbation? How do you do it without thinking about your ex?

Some advice I've heard is to imagine meeting your favorite celebrity and thinking about a tryst with them. Or thinking about an attractive person at work, at the grocery store, etc., basically creating a fantasy with someone else.

Shambo says, "Masturbation after a breakup can be healthy if done mindfully, not to escape emotions or fantasize about the ex. Focus on the sensual feelings versus mental imagery. However, compulsive masturbation to avoid grieving is unwise."

Batista advises, "It's not "unhealthy" to masturbate, it's a natural instinct, when it becomes concerning is if it is hindering your ability to live as a functioning adult in society. It's natural to think about your ex while masturbating in the early stages of a breakup, maybe the sex was amazing, maybe you're romanticizing what's familiar."

"If you are at a point where all you can think about is your ex, and every time you masturbate you start to romanticize the relationship and can't move on, then that's something to self-reflect on. After a breakup, especially a traumatic one, we can tend to negate all the reasons why the relationship didn't work, and just hold on to the positive memories, we crave familiarity—even when if it not healthy/beneficial for us."

So, whether you decide to have sex after your traumatic breakup is entirely up to you and how you feel. But just think about why you're doing it. Remember, you can always "take care of yourself" when you feel the urge. Just try to conjure up a fantasy about someone else—and do it mindfully.

EXERCISE 5:

SET SMALL DAILY GOALS.

Okay, back to the exercises…

When you're going through a breakup, it can be hard to manage your life as you once knew it. The seduction of depression can lure you into your bed and keep you there for days at a time. To stop you from turning into a recluse and losing yourself in the dark black hole of depression, we have come up with an exercise to help you manage your life daily.

This will be an ongoing exercise that you'll ideally perform nightly. You're going to need keep a journal by your bedside for this one.

Perform the following exercise in your personal journal:

Every evening before you go to bed, write down a list of tasks you want to accomplish the following day. These tasks can consist of items such as avoiding contact with

Set Small Daily Goals.

your ex, allowing yourself to break down, promising yourself to cut down on the drinking or smoking, or even focusing on accomplishing a major project at work. The tasks can also be small but significant: keep a dental appointment, visit the grocery store, make a great meal, or push yourself to go to the gym.

The next day, perform all the tasks that you're able to get to. You don't have to do them all but do as many as you feel you can.

At the end of the day, flip back to your entry from the day before and check off the tasks you actually accomplished. If you didn't accomplish a single item on your list, then that's okay. Just add these tasks to your list for tomorrow.

You'll be able to add (and subtract) to this list as you work through the chapters in this book. For example, in Exercise 6 we've laid out a list of healthy foods you can buy in the grocery store (or the convenience store, or Instacart if your motivation-level isn't very high). In Exercise 9, we suggest that you do some interior decorating to change your environment and in Exercise 17, we talk about the importance of working out and harnessing those endorphins to get over your breakup. These aren't exercises that can be done in one evening, so we suggest that as you work through, you add any ideas, shopping lists, and goals to your **Tasks List**.

This may seem like a hassle, but if you're having trouble managing your life at the moment, this will help you stay organized. Accomplishing anything when just the idea of leaving your house seems daunting will help you feel like you're in the "real world" — even if it's just for a minute between sobbing fits or naps. As more time goes by, you will find yourself completing more and more tasks.

EXERCISE 6:
"THE BREAKUP DIET."

There are a lot more healing exercises coming up, but before we get to that, we wanted to check in with you and see what you're eating or not eating. If you have children, you're hopefully at home with a fully stocked refrigerator, but if you're single, who knows what you've got to eat and if you've even eaten recently?

If you're not eating and don't feel like doing full-on grocery shopping, keep reading. We made a cheat-sheet of stuff you can order from Instacart or pick up at the local convenience store so you can zip in, zip out, and get back to the book and your recovery process. Conversely, if you're eating regularly, but perhaps just ordering fast food we urge you to read on as well!

It seems that everyone has a version of "the breakup diet." Whether you lose 10 pounds in a week as a result of not eating and smoking cigarettes, or you gain 20 pounds because you've decided to eat nothing but ice cream for days, not eating or overindulging can devastate your body. According to registered dietician Alicia Romano:

"Poor nutrition can wreak havoc on your overall health and well-being. Lack of the proper nutrients in your diet can leave you feeling more stressed, fatigued, anxious/depressed and can impair your concentration and immune system. Under-nutrition can put you at risk of nutritional deficiencies, dehydration, and can potentially slow your metabolism leading to a rebound in weight gain."

And if you're overeating, Romano says, "On the other extreme, overindulging and weight gain can increase your risk of insulin resistance, putting you at increased risk of being overweight or obese as well as at risk of developing other chronic medical conditions (high blood pressure, high cholesterol, heart disease, Type 2 diabetes, etc.). Although these extreme diet swings may seem like the way to go at the time, they may make your ability to cope and heal from a breakup more difficult. Keeping your body nourished is an essential way to keep your hormones and health in check."

If you're the type of person who completely avoids food while going through a breakup, Romano recommends that you at least make some bare-minimum good choices to reach your baseline nutritional needs:

Take a multivitamin every day, especially if you aren't eating a variety of fresh fruits & vegetables. If you're cutting out essential food groups, it's likely you're not taking in enough! You can do anything from a One A Day® Multivitamin (chewable works) or 2 Flintstones™ Complete MVI with minerals.

Stock up on ready-to-drink nutrition supplements & shakes, especially if you're completely averse to eating food. Some good examples include Ensure®, Muscle Milk®, Carnation® Instant Breakfast and Odwalla® Protein Shakes. Remember, this is NOT a long-term solution, and these shakes should only be used when you really can't stomach "real food." If commercial beverages don't appeal to you, consider making your own nutritious smoothie or shake (see recipe below).

Keep easy-to-grab convenience items on hand so having the right foods to eat is easy and accessible.

Try eating small frequent meals and snacks throughout the day to fill you up, especially if a large meal doesn't appeal to you. Avoid going long hours without eating and try to avoid eating all of your food at one large meal.

Ideally, your diet should consist of a minimum of:

2 Servings of Fruit Per Day	3+ Servings of Veggies Per Day
2+ Servings of Dairy Per Day	4 Servings of Grains & Starches
4 ox Protein Foods	Healthy Fat

Example Convenience Store Grocery List:

- Apples & bananas
- 1 container mixed nuts
- Mini boxes of raisins
- 1 jar of natural peanut butter
- 1 loaf of 100% whole wheat bread
- ½ gallon of low-fat milk
- Kashi® Go Lean Crunch Cereal (or other high fiber, high protein cereal)
- Greek yogurt
- Baby carrots
- Steamer bag of broccoli
- String cheese
- 1 dozen eggs

Example Fast Food Orders:

If fast food is a go-to for you, try to make the healthy choices.

- If you need the fries, stick to a small. Try to avoid, as the heavy fat & sodium content will lead to more bloat!
- Grilled chicken sandwich + apple slices or side salad with light dressing
- Salad with grilled chicken with light dressing
- Junior sized cheeseburgers + apple slices or side salad with light dressing
- Wendy's®: cup of chili + baked potato and/or garden side salad with light dressing
- Wendy's® or Burger King®: veggie burger + apple slices
- Chipotle®: 3 steak or chicken tacos with veggies; hold the cheese
- Chipotle® or Qdoba®: salad bowl with ½ rice, ½ beans, lots of veggies, light on the cheese
- Subway®: 6" on whole wheat bread with turkey or chicken, lots of veggies; serve with apple slices & water or skim milk
- Oatmeal from any fast-food restaurant (such as McDonald's® or Starbucks®)
- Starbucks® protein bistro box or chicken and hummus bistro box

- Starbucks® spinach and feta breakfast wrap
- Dunkin' Donuts® Egg + cheese on English muffin

Example of Simple & Easy Meals:

- 2 eggs scrambled with thawed frozen spinach with toast
- ½ turkey sandwich + 1 string cheese + baby carrots + hummus
- Greek yogurt topped with sliced banana and whole grain cereal
- Peanut butter banana sandwich + celery sticks
- Oatmeal made with low fat milk topped with raisins + chopped nuts
- Veggie burger patty on toasted English muffin with steamer bag of broccoli

Healthy Eating Tips:

Yes, we know, you're going through a breakup and the last thing you want to do is read about food. But it's really important that you eat well, because it can help keep your emotions in check. Think about how you feel when you have low blood sugar, or how crabby you can get when you're starving. This is part of the reason we've included this chapter.

Romano says, "You will see we are stressing healthy eating, choosing foods that nourish your body, keep you energized and stabilize your emotional roller coaster. Tacking on unhealthy, mood-busting foods that are highly processed, high in saturated and trans-fat, high in sugar and sodium will not only expand your waistline, but they may also make any emotional swings worse! It's easy to emotionally eat and turn to comfort foods: chips, fried foods, desserts & pastries, but at the end of the day you're going to be left feeling worse."

To combat emotional eating, Romano recommends the following:

Stay hydrated! This will keep you energized, help fight fatigue and limit dehydration! This will also help regulate your metabolism. Try to take in about eight 8oz glasses of water per day. You don't need Gatorade; to zest up your water, add lemon or lime juice, cucumbers, berries, etc. Try flavored soda water, such as Polar Seltzer or Poland Springs sparkling water.

Cut Back on Added Sugar! Sugary sweet things may seem comforting at the time of encounter, but they will leave you feeling dull and tired within an hour! Cut back on added sugars found in regular soda, juice & other sugar sweetened beverages; limit candies and processed sweets with added sugar; Keep your sweet treats to one serving per day to avoid swings in your blood sugars which may lead to swings in your mood!

Limit caffeine. Try to limit caffeine as much as you can, as this will leave you dehydrated! Don't rely on caffeine to pick up your energy, as it will only be a quick fix. Two 8oz cups of coffee is a suitable limit; switch to decaf coffee or decaf tea if able; avoid energy drinks like Red Bull® as well as diet soda; If you're feeling the urge for coffee or a caffeine boost, try drinking 8oz of water & having a small snack (such as an apple + a string cheese); this may leave you more energized!

Pair all meals & snacks with a protein. Choose lean proteins when able (i.e. 90% cuts of ground meat, or boneless skinless poultry); avoid highly processed meats & cheeses when able; if choosing lunch meat, ask for low sodium varieties.

Limit highly processed foods as much as possible. Here's a general rule of thumb: if the ingredient list is longer than your grocery list and contains more than 1-3 ingredients that you can't pronounce or recognize, put that food down.

Limit refined carbohydrates. Nix the white pasta, white bread, crackers, and chips that aren't whole grain; stick to 100% whole wheat/whole grain varieties of starches & grains when possible.

Stay away from trans-fat. If you see trans-fat or "partially hydrogenated oil" on the ingredients list, put it down. On top of it, limit the highly fatty foods, especially those that are fried.

Limit your sodium intake. Choose unsalted varieties of nuts or pretzels; stay away from full sodium varieties of soup or cold cuts- look for labels that say "low sodium" when possible. A general rule of thumb, choose items with <500mg of sodium per serving.

The moral of the story? Romano says, "Try to find some kind of balance. Get your nutrition from real food. Eat your fruit, vegetables, grains, and dairy. Try to balance your meals and snacks by combining food groups. Limit highly processed foods as much as you can, but if needed for convenience, stick to those that we outlined on the list above. Remember, the foods you eat will play a large role on your emotions—do yourself a favor and avoid starchy, sugary, salty, and overly fatty foods that will bust your mood."

Add "shopping" to your **Tasks List** and consider some healthy options in addition to sweet treats & junk food.

EXERCISE 7:

WRITE DOWN THE THINGS YOU LOVED.

While you're getting over your ex and going through an inevitable withdrawal period, subconsciously you'll likely magnify your ex's good qualities. In your head, you'll build your ex up so much that you'll honestly believe that you'll never find another lover quite as good, you'll never meet someone who makes you laugh as hard, and you'll never find someone quite as charming.

In simple terms, you've put your ex on a pedestal. So, we're going to take that energy and eventually push it inward so you're not so focused on the ex. Let's do the work to kick your former love off that pedestal, shall we?

Write Down The Things You Loved.

To heal, you're going to have to re-live your relationship from the beginning. Although painful, these exercises will help you remember the good times and the bad. Your ex is just a human who decided with or without your consent that it's time to move on without you. Just one person who decided that you were not "the one." Yes, it sucks, but your ex is just a human—one out of the thousands of humans you could've been dating. Try to remember that.

The next few exercises are meant to gauge your feelings as they stand currently. Later in the book, we will analyze these exercises and prove that your ex may not have been as great of a fit for you as you thought.

List up to 10 things you loved about your ex.

1. _____

   _____

   _____

2. _____

   _____

   _____

3. _____

   _____

   _____

4. _____

   _____

   _____

5. _____
   _____
   _____

6. _____
   _____
   _____

7. _____
   _____
   _____

8. _____
   _____
   _____

9. _____
   _____
   _____

10. _____
    _____
    _____

That was probably tough, sorry. Take some time here to cry if you need to. More thought-provoking exercises that may tug at your heartstrings are coming up.

EXERCISE 8:

QUESTION YOUR RELATIONSHIP.

So, on the tail of asking you to write down the 10 things you loved about your ex, we're now going to ask you to reminisce about your relationship. It may seem cruel, but according to past readers, this can be one of the most useful exercises in this book because it compels you to focus on your feelings about your relationship. It can be so easy to sweep issues under the carpet, so this exercise forces you to think about them.

Let's travel back in time to when all things seemed perfect.

Answer these questions as honestly as you can. If you find yourself writing the word "but" a lot, it could mean that you are excusing the behavior. This is about you. Write how you felt honestly about these situations to help yourself heal.

Alright, let's get to it. Take some time to answer these questions about your relationship. It may seem exhausting to answer all of these questions at once, so take all the time you need to complete this exercise.

How did you two meet?

_____
_____
_____
_____

Where did you meet?

_____
_____
_____
_____

Where did you go on your first date?

_____
_____
_____
_____

In general, were you picked up for dates?

_____
_____
_____
_____

How did this make you feel?

_____
_____
_____
_____

What about your ex attracted you the most?

_____
_____
_____
_____

When and where did you have your first kiss?

_____
_____
_____
_____

Was it romantic? Why or why not?

_____
_____
_____
_____

Did you meet your ex's friends?

_____
_____
_____
_____

If not, how did that make you feel?

Did you meet your ex's friends?

What did you think of them?

Did your ex meet your friends?

What did your friends think of your ex?

How did your ex treat your friends?

_____
_____
_____
_____

Did you meet the ex's family?

_____
_____
_____
_____

If not, how did that make you feel?

_____
_____
_____
_____

What did you think of your ex's family?

_____
_____
_____
_____

What do you think they thought of you?

_____
_____
_____
_____

How was your relationship with your ex's family?

_____
_____
_____
_____

Did your ex meet your family?

_____
_____
_____
_____

If so, did your ex like/get along with your family?

_____
_____
_____
_____

How did that make you feel?

_____
_____
_____
_____

Did you sleep with your ex?

_____
_____
_____
_____

Be honest, how was sex on a scale of 1 to 10?

_____
_____
_____
_____

Who initiated sex more?

_____
_____
_____
_____

How did that make you feel?

_____
_____
_____
_____

After sex, did you cuddle or talk?

_____
_____
_____
_____

How did that make you feel? Was it what you wanted?

_____
_____
_____
_____

Was your ex affectionate in public?

_____
_____
_____
_____

Did you like that, or did you wish it were different?

_____
_____
_____
_____

Do you think you could have changed that?

_____
_____
_____
_____

Was your ex reliable?

_____
_____
_____

Do you feel that your ex always told you the truth?

_____
_____
_____

Why or why not?

_____
_____
_____

What did your ex do for a living?

_____
_____
_____

Did you have any concerns about your ex's job?

_____
_____
_____

Who called or texted more frequently? Your ex? You?

_____
_____
_____
_____

Do you wish that would have been different?

_____
_____
_____
_____

Overall, who initiated contact more?

_____
_____
_____
_____

And how did that make you feel?

_____
_____
_____
_____

Did your ex celebrate your birthday(s) with you?

_____
_____
_____
_____

Did you have to remind them it was your birthday?

_____
_____
_____

Did they buy you a gift or do something nice for you?

_____
_____
_____

If so, was said gift/gesture romantic in nature?

_____
_____
_____

How did that make you feel?

_____
_____
_____

Did your ex ever do anything for you "just because?"

_____
_____
_____

Did your ex attend your special events with you?

Did your ex invite you to their special events?

Which events? (Anything involving coworkers, family?)

Were you proud to be with your ex?

What is the nicest thing they ever did for you?

_____
_____
_____
_____

What is the nicest thing you ever did for your ex?

_____
_____
_____
_____

Did you or your ex pay for more dates?

_____
_____
_____
_____

If so, did that bother you?

_____
_____
_____
_____

Did your ex support you financially or vice-versa?

_____

_____

_____

If so, did that bother you? Why or why not?

_____

_____

_____

Did you and your ex say, "I love you" to one another?

_____

_____

_____

If so, who said it first?

_____

_____

_____

If not, do you regret not saying it?

_____
_____
_____
_____

How long were you together?

_____
_____
_____
_____

Did you break up more than once?

_____
_____
_____
_____

How did you break up this final time?

_____
_____
_____
_____

Why did you break up this final time?

Did you feel that you could depend on your ex?

How did that make you feel? Secure or insecure?

Did your ex cheat on you?

If so, how did you find out?

Do you think they would cheat on you again?

How does this make you feel?

Did you feel you could really trust your ex?

If you did, but then lost it, why?

Do you think you could trust your ex again?

Is your perception of the relationship changing now?

All of those questions, though painful to answer right now, are supposed to help you gauge your relationship and how it actually was. Sometimes you get so caught up in a feeling you had at the very beginning of a relationship (that giddy feeling with butterflies in your stomach), that you actually spend the real "meat" of your relationship trying to recapture that feeling.

If, after answering these questions, you managed to find that you were in a truly good relationship, that's actually good news. It means that you're able to pick someone who was able to give you the things you desire in a relationship, instead of chasing after a phantom feeling. It also is understandable why it's been hard for you to move on.

So, whether your relationship was a good one, or whether you're starting to see the flaws that were existent, we want you to think about this exercise. What other questions can you ask yourself about the relationship? And would the answers please you? Or would they make you see more flaws?

EXERCISE 9:
MAKE YOUR PLACE YOUR OWN AGAIN.

Chances are that everything in your place reminds you of your ex. This is the chair in which they liked to sit. This is the couch where you guys used to make out. These are the sheets on your bed on which there are traces of their cheap, drugstore perfume or cologne. Okay, so maybe it was expensive perfume or cologne, and it smells divine, but the point is that it's going to be very hard to let go if you can still see and smell your ex everywhere. And that's why it's time to make some changes!

Now it's time to make your place your own again; and no matter your gender, this exercise is an important one. Just read through it and choose what works for you.

For most people, buying all new furniture every time a relationship ends is not an option, but there are some thrifty things you can do to make changes in your home. So, we went to the experts! Interior designer Samantha Scott offers some advice for those who want to make a quick change without breaking the bank, "Paint, paint, paint! Changing the wall color will have a dramatic impact on the space. If you are renting, and painting is not an option, change your window treatments to freshen up and transform your room."

We've made it easy to help you revamp your space, by giving tips on a room-by-room basis. As you go through each room, we suggest taking a big box or bag with you, so you can put everything that either reminds you of (or belongs to) your former love in there; every photo, every piece of clothing — absolutely everything. When you're finished, you'll find a place to put that box or bag so it will be out of the way. Whether it's the basement, a closet, or even a trusted friend or family member's home – you'll want this stuff out of sight for the time being.

In terms of decorating, we suggest that you do as little or as much as makes you comfortable.

The point of this exercise is to reclaim your space. Scott adds, "Everywhere we go, everything we touch, we leave a piece of our energy behind — as does our ex. Cleansing your space by removing negative energy allows you to create a positive environment. This is your time to take back your space not just physically or environmentally but more importantly, emotionally, and mentally. The goal is to remove any and everything having to do with your ex-partner, including items you brought with you into the home that now remind you of your past relationship. Your ideal space should be the right balance of your personality and an extension of your heart and creativity."

She also suggests decorating with positive quotes and mantras to help change the energy in your space, "I've always found it

inspiring to creatively leave positive affirmations throughout the home. Whether framing a favorite quote or simply sticking to a pin board or on the inside of your closet door, it's yet another great way to bring in the much-needed positive energy you long for reminding you that 'Yes You Can'!"

Here's what you can do in different rooms of your domicile to help you make your place your own again:

In the kitchen:

When you think about your ex, you probably don't think too much about items in the kitchen. Well, that's why you got this book; we don't want you to end up digging around in the refrigerator three weeks from now, coming across a particular brand of salsa or cheese you purchased just for your ex, bringing back memories and ruining your progress. So, take this time to get rid of those kinds of things.

Give unopened items to charity, give them to your friends, or simply throw them out. Purging is good! Plus, you'll need room in your fridge to put all the new, healthy food you purchased in your journey to take control of and successfully manage "The Breakup Diet"!

Interior Designer, Samantha Scott adds, "When working towards changing the energy in your kitchen, you may feel limited as to what you can do. However, there are many simple projects you can do on your own to inspire and help create more positive energy."

Scott's kitchen tips:

If you have a table and chairs in the kitchen and purchasing new furniture is not an option, add slipcovers to your chairs to transform the space. It's amazing that adding something as simple as a chair slipcover can help create the illusion an entirely new kitchen set!

When space allows, change it up a bit. Something as simple as moving your table at an angle can change the energy in the room.

Treat yourself to new glassware and or flatware. I'm all too familiar with how pieces are 'lost' (like a favorite glassware set or special set of knives) when ending a relationship.

Clear off your counter tops. Try your best to keep the area free of the unnecessary items we often leave on our counters, such as mail and even kitchen utensils we may no longer use. If these items are in use, store them in a pantry or cabinet.

Treat yourself to fresh flowers every so often. In my neighborhood, we have a supermarket that sells the most beautiful, long lasting, inexpensive roses. At times they've lasted 3-4 weeks! Anytime I have a visitor, I'm complimented on how pretty the flowers are.

In the bedroom:

The bedroom is probably going to be the harshest reminder of your ex. There may be clothing, photos of the two of you, and let's just not even think of the physical things that happened in the bed itself. If you haven't done so already, grab anything tangible that you can, clothing (clean out closets, dressers and don't forget to dig through the hamper), photos, cards, etc., and put everything in the box. Can't fit everything? Get another box!

Next, make small changes in your bedroom. Interior Designer Samantha Scott offers this advice:

"If your budget allows—go for it—buy that bed or mattress you've had your eye on. This could be anything from a wooden sleigh bed to a new memory foam mattress. What's important is it is a reflection of your personality and the new space you're creating."

It's always nice to bring some change by purchasing a new comforter set, sheets and pillows. This is a great way to express your personality and it is always fun shopping for bedding.

Re-arranging your space is going to go a long way. Change it up! Shake up the stale negative energy and allow the positive to start to flow. This can be as simple as repositioning a mirror or completely moving your bed and dresser.

The bedroom is the most personal space in your home—make it about you.

In the bathroom:

Go through your cabinets, shelves, and shower and find your ex's toothpaste, shower gel, soap, razor, etc. Either throw it all away or put it in the box to give to your ex at a later date.

Next, transform the space and make it your own. Interior designer Samantha Scott offers these easy instructions:

"Once you've cleaned out your cabinets and drawers, treat yourself to a new shower curtain. If you don't want to replace the curtain be sure to wash it and make it your own again."

"Purchasing something as small as new hand soap dispenser or hand towels and creatively stacking them on the counter will add an extra element to the space, reflecting more of your style."

In the common areas:

Take one more sweep of your home and pick out and remove key things that remind you of your ex. For example, put away a certain blanket you used to cuddle under together on your living room couch and temporarily replace it with a different one. Next, follow these great design tips from Scott:

"In your living or family room, if allowed, paint, paint, and paint! Once again, this is a great start to transforming your room's energy. Choosing a color that best suits you will really connect you to your space making you want to spend time there."

"Plants are great as 'filler'. Not only do they produce oxygen, but plants also suck up negative energy still lingering that can be toxic to your ability to move forward."

"Create ambiance with lighting. Simple changes such as adding a new lamp or installing a new ceiling fixture can change the room. Choose an option that best complements your style."

"If space allows, reposition your couch, television, and any other furniture you may have in there. Be aware when moving your furniture of how you feel the energy is flowing throughout the room."

Finally, clean up, catch up on laundry, and dust off your furniture. You can do all of this instead of wasting away in front of the television. You will feel better if you can mope about in a clean house. We know it sounds strange, but it's true. At least you will have accomplished something and that always feels good.

Right now, you are taking your life back from your ex. These small symbolic changes will help you make your life your own again.

If you're moving out of the home you shared with your ex (or even if your ex is moving out), the same rules apply. Do whatever you can to jettison those memories from your new place. This exercise should take you a few evenings. Shopping can prove to be therapeutic but try not to overspend. You are upset as it is right now—there's no sense in overextending your budget too.

Bring in the professionals!

But if you do have the budget to hire an interior decorator (and maybe it's something you've been thinking about for a while), Samantha Scott gives this advice on hiring a designer:

"Hiring a designer is a big decision. If your budget allows, bringing in a designer is great way to start the transformation of your space. Pricing can vary depending on what you are looking to do. You'll find designers may charge an hourly rate while others will charge a percentage of the items they purchased for the home, in addition to charging an hourly rate. For a more sizable project, it's not uncommon for a designer to charge a percentage of the total merchandise purchased without billing an hourly rate."

Once you've decided you're ready to bring in a professional, Scott offers the following advice to identify if they're a good fit for you:

"It's important to know you're being listened to. Is this person asking questions about you, your likes and why you're looking to make changes?"

"Communication is huge. Essentially you are putting your trust in this person. Ensure that they are hearing you and really understand your personality, sense of style and what makes you tick."

"Whether or not this person is a referral from family or a friend, take a look at their website, their portfolio. It's not about finding a designer with your 'exact' taste as much as it is about choosing someone with an appreciation for all styles from classic to contemporary."

"When meeting with this person, see if you are getting a good vibe. Are they bringing in their own positive energy?"

Scott says, "Once you've zoned in a couple of designers, go with the one who makes you feel great just by speaking with them. This will undoubtedly translate into to their work, leaving you with the refreshed, positive environment you're looking for to move forward and begin your journey."

And finally, Scott offers one last piece of advice, "It's time for your fresh new journey and it begins with surrounding yourself with positive energy. Let this cleanse be the one that changes your life.

Take this opportunity to learn who you are. You make the decision as to what you're willing to compromise — no more sacrificing what's truly important to you.

No more allowing negative energy to rob you of your passions. This is your life. YOU are now in a position to choose your surroundings and create your perfect environment."

We couldn't have said it better!

Perform a Sage Ritual:

Burning sage (also known as smudging) is a practice that dates back to prehistoric times and is used to cleanse a person, group of people, or space. People believe the smoke removes bad feelings or bad energy from a place. It is thought. to cleanse the body, mind, and spirit, promoting balance and harmony.

Perform this ancient ritual with care (because it's fire!).

1. Open windows:

    Let stagnant energy leave by opening windows to allow airflow.

2. Set an intention:

    Consider what you want to achieve with the ritual, such as welcoming a new beginning or releasing stagnant energy (or releasing your ex!).

3. Light the sage:

   Hold the sage at a 45-degree angle above a flame, like a candle. Let it burn for about 20 seconds, then gently blow out the flame.

4. Walk around:

   Carry the sage around your home, encouraging the smoke into all spaces. Give special attention to areas in front of mirrors, corners, and spaces like entrances, hallways, and doorways.

5. Put out the sage:

   When you're all done, push the burning end into your clay bowl or fireproof vessel.

EXERCISE 10:
WRITING TO HEAL.

In this exercise, we're going to talk about a process called "expressive writing," created by renowned psychologist Dr. James Pennebaker. As part of this process, Dr. Pennebaker asks that for 20 minutes, over a period of four days, a person write about their deepest emotional upheaval that is influencing their life the most. He stresses about the importance of letting go, exploring the event and its overall effect on a person's life. He even suggests tying the experience to your childhood, the relationship with your parents, people you have loved (or love now), or your job/career.

In his book <u>Writing to Heal</u>, Pennebaker states, "People who engage in expressive writing report feeling happier and less negative than before writing. Similarly, reports of depressive symptoms, rumination, and general anxiety tend to drop in the weeks and months after writing about emotional upheavals."

Either use the journal our purchased or use a different pad of paper to perform this emotional writing exercise. Set time to do it every day for four days (in a row) for 20 minutes a day.

Write about the biggest emotional upheaval in your life. It could be the death of a loved one, your parents' divorce, or it could be something completely different. As you write, think about it in terms of how this has affected all of your romantic relationships, and even the most current one.

You don't have to stop at this point for 4 days. You can continue to the next exercise and do it while you're performing this exercise. Just be sure to add "expressive writing" to your **Tasks List** for the next 4 days and really take the time to explore the depth and breadth of your feelings.

EXERCISE 11:
GET IN TOUCH WITH YOUR SPIRITUAL SIDE.

Whether it's yoga, meditation, or attending church or temple, now may be a great time to get in touch with your spiritual side. This includes learning gratitude and focusing on self-care in order to heal.

On self-care, Chanelle Camire, Registered Yoga Teacher and founder of Sweet Balance Life & Style Consulting (https://www.sweetbalanceyoga.com/) says, "Beginning a yoga or mediation practice is crucial for creating a relationship with yourself which is where a great deal of your healing will come from."

She goes on to say, "When going through difficult times, especially paralyzing moments of heartbreak and loss, you must listen to what your body needs to share. The more time you can spend listening, the more grounding you'll experience. You'll become more fine-tuned with what you need to heal. It's not about shutting our minds off but rather being aware of what's coming up and letting it go, letting it go and continuously letting it all go."

But it's not going to all happen at once. Camire says, "Your mind is going to bait you. It's going to replay all of the wonderful moments and make that grip tighter. That bait will trick you to believe lies just to keep you holding on. And that's where Yoga and meditation come in. They will teach you to let go and regain control over yourself. You'll learn to trust your gut because you'll create sensitivity for your needs. When the thoughts come up look at them, smile and then let them go. You just keep coming back to your breath. You connect to the moment. What can you hear? What can you smell? What's the temperature of the air? You just keep plugging back in. Before you know it, you'll wake up one day and everything will be ok. I promise. You just have to train yourself. It's like biting your nails. You have to be conscious. The more you can love yourself to not hold onto what doesn't serve you, the quicker you'll be able to say 'next!' and be open to another experience."

Finally, Camire advises, "Yoga prepares your body for mediation, so start slowly when adding both into your life. I recommend you take as many classes and meet as many teachers as you can. You want to be able to use your yoga and meditation like a prescription. You'll know what you need and where to go depending on your circumstances. I've practiced Yoga since I was 8 and it's amazing, but meditation is what changed my life in the most magical ways. Get on your mat. Take a deep breath and let it all go."

If you can't afford to take classes or don't have time to do a guided meditation with an instructor, we have good news for you. There are many kinds of free meditational exercises and beginner's Yoga practices available on YouTube. Take some time off from your worry and anxiety and explore what's available to you. A sound mind and a connection with yourself will help you grow stronger and heal from your breakup.

Add to your **Tasks List** that you'll at least try one YouTube, Headspace, or Calm guided meditation practice and set time aside to do it within the week. None of the exercises in this book will actually help unless you do them. If you hate it, or find that it doesn't relax you, then seek out something else that works for you.

In fact, to make it easier on you, here are some items that we think can help!

Yoga with Adriene on YouTube is hands-down my favorite Yoga teacher. She does everything from short classes to long classes, covering beginners and experienced yoga practitioners.

Meditate. Guided meditation has helped me tremendously. If you visit YouTube, or download Headspace, you'll find thousands of meditation exercises. Find one that is right for you.

Download the Calm app or the Headspace App. These are Mental Fitness apps, famous for guided meditations, sleep stories, relaxing music, and more.

EXERCISE 12:

SELF-SOOTHE TO HEAL.

Throughout this book, we've been talking about embracing your pain, changing your environment, and entering a "healing cocoon" of sorts while you get through the emotions related to this breakup. This is an exercise that's an extension of those ideas.

Lisa Bahar, licensed marriage and family therapist and licensed professional clinical counselor who specializes in Dialectical Behavior Therapy (DBT) and healthy relationship building, www.lisabahar.com, recommends a process of self-soothing. She says, "Self-soothing is part of the process of comforting yourself and tending to yourself by activating and engaging the 5 senses. In this process you'll learn how to be with your emotions rather than rejecting them and you'll become your own internal comforter."

So, if you are your own internal comforter, it means that you're not turning to someone else to make you feel better (yes, we're talking to you, person who thinks that the best way to get over someone is to get under someone else). And instead of blaming yourself and punishing yourself (as many of us tend to do when a relationship ends), you actually care for yourself, treat yourself and calm yourself.

So, say you're uncomfortable dealing with your emotions, or you're afraid to feel them. Or maybe instead of allowing yourself to deal with a problem that seems overwhelming, you drink too much or engage in other self-destructive behavior (one-night stands). With self-soothing, instead of doing something that could be harmful to your person, you do something that's comforting and nurturing. You'll take a time-out and allow yourself to enjoy something using 1, 2, or all 5 of your senses whenever you feel stressed or upset.

The process of self-soothing is designed to put yourself in a comfortable state of being and allowing your emotions to be present if they occur. Bahar says, "If pain comes forth, notice it, breathe, and allow the emotions to occur. Self-soothing creates a kind of warmth that surrounds the individual as they comfort themselves."

So, here are some ideas for you to self-soothe when you're feeling overwhelmed with negative emotions and feelings during this recovery period.

Visual: Create a visual environment that is pleasing to the eye, this may include flowers, candles, lighting that is softer, paintings that are soothing, sculptures or other decorations in your environment that are pleasing to your visual eye.

Scent/Smell: Add soothing and pleasing scents to your environment. It could be scented flowers, herbs, sea salt sprays, aromatherapy or oils, cup of tea that smells soothing, or freshly washed clothes out of the dryer.

Touch: Touch something that soothes you. It could be a soft pillow, a favorite comforter, an animal that you pet (like a cat or a dog), the touch of velvet, anything that feels good to the touch, including a bubble bath, or shower.

Hearing: Add soothing sounds to your environment. This includes music that has a neutral calming effect, tweeting birds, waves, or wind chimes. You could also take time to do a meditation exercise from YouTube (or on tape, mp3, CD or DVD).

Taste: This isn't about emotional eating; it's about taking pleasure in something that tastes good to you. For example, a healthy ripe fruit, coffee the way you like it, a cold drink, a healthy snack, or cup of tea.

Then a **Multisensory Experience** would include the combination of all of these:

- Take a soothing, lavender-scented bubble bath with candles, music, a cup of tea and a warm towel or bathrobe.

- Go to the beach, get on a raft (or go surfing!) drink a cool glass of iced tea, listen to the waves, feel the sand underneath your feet, or the beach towel on your body, and notice the scent of the sea salt.

About this process, Bahar says, "The key is to notice the senses being activated and being mindful and engaging your sensory process, which is the way the body and the mind heal. Get in touch with the elements."

So, if you're not near a beach, or a boat, then take some time to figure out your own ways to self-soothe. Here's an easy one:

- Light some candles
- Make a cup of chamomile tea
- Turn on some soothing music
- Run some hot water in your bathtub
- Add lavender-scented bubbles

Enjoy the warm water, really allow yourself to smell the lavender, delight in the taste of the tea and if any feelings of sadness come, allow yourself to feel them. If they don't come, just allow yourself to take pleasure in the small comforts. This will help you manage your stress, come to terms with your feelings and help heal your heart.

EXERCISE 13:

WRITE A LETTER TO YOUR EX (BUT DON'T SEND IT!).

You have now had some time to reflect upon the breakup. Now it's time to write a letter to your ex. You're not going to mail it or send it. This is just for you. Write down all of your feelings as you have them. Write down why you are upset. Write down what you want. And most importantly, don't hold back.

Psychotherapist Cynthia C. McKay, J.D., M.A. says, "Any kind of "narrative therapy" can be cathartic. Knowing the letter is "safe" with no intent to mail or email, I would suggest writing a letter to the ex with absolutely no editing or suppression of speech—just pour your heart out! State everything that went wrong and why the relationship may have been doomed from the beginning."

The purpose of this letter is twofold. One, you'll get everything out. Two, you'll hopefully see your relationship from a different point of view. As McKay says, "The reality of seeing your thoughts in print can often give a better perspective as to why you may actually be better off now."

And if you feel as if you do need to send it somewhere, mail it to yourself or save it in your drafts folder, or just email it to yourself.

One thing McKay suggests is writing your letter on a few sheets of paper and then shredding or burning those sheets "in order to complete the ritual." Doing so, she says, "will bring actual closure to the event."

When writing your letter, you have our full permission to use curse words. Just get it all out in a way that makes sense to you and reflects your feelings.

EXERCISE 14:

SING

We know, we know. When you're in the throes of a breakup, you want to listen to your sad songs, because at least they speak to your pain. Jennifer Klesman, licensed therapist and author of <u>You Can't Stay There, Surviving a Breakup One Moment at a Time</u> says, "Breakup songs can be so validating when we're struggling," and she's more of an advocate of listening to them when they feel good, and then gradually switch. She goes on to say, "We may not want life to move on at first, so let the playlist be filled with sad songs, but gradually add more of the upbeat ones."

So, go ahead and start with the sad songs. But when you're ready, add some upbeat songs to your playlist and put it on shuffle. This way, Klesman says, "you'll give your pain space and then get some energy and dance/sing to the next song."

Eventually, switch your playlist to even more upbeat songs to help you stay focused on recovery during your commute, trips to the grocery store, or just picking up your children. Everyone has their own style of music but try to choose songs that make you feel good.

Here are some examples we've picked out for you as a starter:

- "Happy" by Pharrell Williams
- "Fighter" by Christina Aguilera
- "The Middle" by Jimmy Eat World
- "Since U Been Gone" by Kelly Clarkson
- "Stronger" by Kelly Clarkson
- "Survivor" by Destiny's Child
- "I Will Survive" by Gloria Gaynor
- "I Am Woman" by Helen Reddy
- "I Don't Miss You At All" by Selena Gomez
- "Forget You" by Cee Lo Green
- "Damnit" by Blink182
- "Song for the Dumped" by Ben Folds Five
- "We Are Never Getting Back Together" by Taylor Swift
- "Flowers" by Miley Cyrus
- "Gives you Hell" by All American Rejects

- The entire "Lemonade" album by Beyonce
- "Thank You, Next" by Ariana Grande

Now take some time to curate your own playlist with songs that speak to your heart and soul. Use these songs to create a sense of empowerment as you move forward on your journey.

EXERCISE 15:

VISIT THE PAST.

Now make a plan to accomplish this exercise: Take time to go near/drive by your previous boyfriend or girlfriend's house, or a place you used to hang out—like a coffee shop, a club, or a place you used to frequently eat. (Not your current ex—but one before this breakup). It may be someone you haven't thought of in years but make it someone who was important to you.

You may think it's crazy to suggest this but hear us out.

Get to/near the place you've chosen and try to remember how it felt when you guys broke up. Were you heartbroken? Did you think you would never get over it or love again? Did you feel that your life was over when this relationship ended? How does it feel being there now?

The hope is that it doesn't even faze you to be there in this moment. That you're completely ambivalent as opposed to being a complete basket case.

Does this give you just a little bit of perspective about what you're going through now? It should.

You went through this feeling before, you emerged, and you rose like a phoenix from the ashes. You were strong enough to get through complete heartache before and you are strong enough to do it again.

How do you feel after visiting the past?

___
___
___
___
___
___
___
___
___
___
___
___
___
___
___
___
___
___
___
___
___
___

EXERCISE 16:

USE ANGER AS A CRUTCH.

You've now done 15 (!!!) exercises aimed at helping you put your relationship in perspective and getting your independence back.

While you're trying to get a handle on your feelings to feel normal again, perhaps there's also a bit of frustration welling up inside of you. Logically your brain is telling you that you'll be okay, but your heart just isn't on board. You used to be happy, but now possibly you're beginning to get a bit angry about everything—the time you spent and invested in this person, the future that you now have to throw away, the failed expectations, and more! You may not think of yourself as an angry person, but sometimes, anger is what can get you through the hard times. Anger can get you over the hump. Anger can help you get over your ex.

Karen Steinberg, LCSW and Founder of The Possibility Practice (https://thepossibilitypractice.com/) says, "Many people think that being angry means being destructive, either to themselves or to other people and things. There are many other options. The key to getting better is using whatever you have at your disposal, including anger, to reignite your creative capacity to build your life. Most of us need help to do this, whether it is from a book, friends, or a therapy group, as it is hard to do on your own."

And since you've chosen a workbook as part of your healing program, we're including a few exercises to help you use any anger you may be feeling as you heal in a constructive manner.

Psychotherapist Cynthia C. McKay, J.D., M.A. says a helpful writing exercise goes like this, "place every annoying, hurtful, and rude incident on paper while stipulating each emotion you felt as you were subject to the action. Review the list and you may be surprised at how much dysfunction you feel. Don't you feel better already?"

With this in mind, write down these negative occurrences, and then take a moment to write down the emotions you felt while going through them. For example, if you or your ex had a particularly nasty argument last summer, did you feel scared? Angry? Upset?

Negative Occurrence:

_____
_____
_____

How did this negative occurrence make you feel?

_____
_____
_____

Negative Occurrence:

_____
_____
_____

How did this negative occurrence make you feel?

_____
_____
_____

Negative Occurrence:

_____
_____
_____

How did this negative occurrence make you feel?

___

Negative Occurrence:

___

How did this negative occurrence make you feel?

___

Negative Occurrence:

___

How did this negative occurrence make you feel?

___

Negative Occurrence:

_____
_____
_____
_____

How did this negative occurrence make you feel?

_____
_____
_____
_____

Now scream at the top of your lungs. Pound your fists into a pillow. Take a long run. Take a self-defense class. Learn boxing. Do whatever it is that you have to do to get this anger out instead of letting it fester.

Feel a little better to get that out? It does feel good to get angry at times, so every time you're angry with your ex, with the situation, with everything…write down your feelings. Write down your revenge fantasies. Write down words you've only dreamed of using. Anger is an emotion that requires an outlet. It diminishes when you can get it all out of your system. Clearly, writing it once may not do it all, but writing your feelings down will help.

EXERCISE 17:

EXERCISE TO HEAL.

Now that you've made an upbeat playlist and you've gotten a little bit angry, why not use both things together to fuel your workouts?

We're not telling you to work out because it will help you lose weight. We're not telling you to work out because it will help your self-esteem. We're not telling you to work out because it will help you focus on work.

We're telling you to work out because you need an outlet for your stress and anger. We're telling you to work out because it's time to get off your rear end and back into the real world.

But for added incentive, when you exercise, your body produces endorphins or natural opiates that make you feel good. Exercise can trigger happiness, tranquility, euphoria, and creativity that will last from a few minutes to 24 hours.

Timothy LeaTrea, NCSA-CPT says, "Endorphins are neurotransmitters that the brain releases to alleviate pain. This release is more commonly known as a 'runner's high.' Group fitness classes such as yoga, Zumba, or Pilates have been shown to have a greater effect on the release of these endorphins. By simply exercising for a minimum of twenty minutes per day, three days per week you can improve mood and self-esteem without medication."

But what if you don't currently belong to a gym and finding a trainer seems daunting? LeaTrea offers this advice, "Picking a trainer is like any relationship; anything will work for the short term, but a good match gets the best results. Ask prospective trainers questions; find out what they specialize in, what their credentials are, policies on cancellations, and any other questions you might have. Our job is to provide clients with information and guidance perspective trainers should be forth coming with information and policies. Essentially you are interviewing someone who is going to (hopefully) have a major impact on your life."

LeaTrea also talks about settling down with a good gym, "Selecting a gym also takes some consideration, you don't want to go to a bodybuilding gym for a Zumba class. Do your homework, find a gym that fits your needs and budget. A little extra time will help you to be happier with your trainer and your gym."

So, get out of your rut and start exercising! Not only will you start to feel better, but you'll definitely start to look better as well.

And while you're at it, ask a friend to work out with you. It's easier to stay motivated to work out if you employ the "buddy system." And let's face it: it's more fun to scope out hot gym bodies with a friend than all by your lonesome.

Take a moment to write down at least one of your exercise goals. For example, you could write, "I would like to lose 2 inches around my waist," or "I would like to be able to run one mile without stopping." Or "I would like to try to work out 3x a week, no matter how many minutes I spend at the gym."

1. _____
_____
_____
_____
_____

2. _____
_____
_____
_____
_____

3. _____
_____
_____
_____
_____

4. _____
_____
_____
_____
_____

5. _____
_____
_____
_____
_____

6. _____
_____
_____
_____
_____

Then, after you've met with your trainer, or have visited the gym, or started with an online yoga practice, or perhaps Peloton, design some ways to reach your exercise goals.

Add "working out" to your **Tasks List**.

EXERCISE 18:
ANALYZE IT.

Refer to exercise 5 of this book. Read your list of "The 10 things you loved about your ex." Dissect your list and see if any of the things you loved had anything to do with the way your former love treated you. We made up some examples to help you analyze it. We'll go through ours first:

1. My ex was funny

2. My ex co-founded a software company

3. My ex had a lot of friends

4. My ex owned a home

5. My ex liked to travel

6. My ex made me laugh

7. My ex was a good kisser

8. My ex drove a nice car

9. My ex was outgoing

10. My ex liked to try new places to eat

As you can see by our list, none of these items have anything to do with character. No descriptors, such as: kind, caring, attentive, sweet, or even trustworthy were used. If a person were to read this list arbitrarily, they would deduce that this ex is an outgoing, funny, successful person that is a bit adventurous and a good kisser. It's doubtful that a person would deduce this as a list of 10 things a person loved about someone, because the list is superficial at best. Are the things you loved merely superficial?

Psychotherapist Rachel Weinstein, MA, LCPC adds, "Right now, you are likely believing on some level that you've lost the love of your life. The thing is, being in love is directly connected to a phenomenon called "projection," and understanding this may help you get over your breakup."

"Projection is when we believe that we see traits (both good and bad) in someone else that we can't (or aren't willing to) see in ourselves. We do this as a defense mechanism for lots of different reasons. This isn't to say that your ex wasn't or isn't great or horrible or whatever. But it does mean that when we fall in love, a big part of why we feel so amazing is that in some ways we experience being our truest, brightest, selves. Maybe we've never felt cool, and we fall in love with someone we think is cool. We're now in touch with our own "coolness." The thing is, we had that in us all along—we just weren't in touch with it. Losing this person can never take our own strengths away. They are within us. It's just a matter of how much or how little we are in touch with them."

Answer these questions as honestly as you can:

What did I love about the person I was when I was newly in-love with my ex?

_____
_____
_____
_____
_____
_____
_____

What qualities have I always wanted to embody that I felt I finally did when they loved me?

_____
_____
_____
_____
_____
_____
_____

After you've written or at least thought about the answers to Weinstein's questions, go through your list again and see if you can gain any new insight into your attraction for your ex.

_____
_____
_____
_____
_____
_____
_____
_____
_____
_____
_____
_____
_____
_____
_____
_____
_____
_____
_____
_____
_____

EXERCISE 19:
SPEAK WITH A THERAPIST.

You have probably noted that I have quoted quite a few therapists in this book. There's a reason for that: I believe in the power of therapy. Why? When you're down in the dumps it's hard to get perspective. And sometimes it's easier to gain that perspective from a trained professional than a friend. Afterall, it's their job to listen to every single detail.

But what I love is that after I emote, I get valuable feedback and exercises to do in my journal, to help me understand and process my emotions.

Right now, getting mental health care in person can be a bit difficult, but I urge you to try. There are also many options online. I'll list a few here:

Betterhelp.com

Talkspace.com

Brightside.com

Amwell.com

According to the American Psychological Association, here's what you need to know before choosing online therapy:

"Despite the potential benefits, psychologists caution that Web-therapy may not be the best option for everyone or every situation in need of professional support. Here are some points to consider:

1. Is the therapist licensed in the state you live?

"Licensing protects you. Therapists and psychotherapists are not legally protected words in most states, meaning anyone can claim to be a therapist… Licensure laws protect you by ensuring only those who are trained and qualified to practice received a license. This ensures you have recourse if there are problems with your treatment."

Is the site or app secure? Will the information I provide remain confidential? "…psychologists ensure that clients have a safe and private space to share deeply personal and sometimes difficult stories." That reassurance can mean everything when it comes to trusting."

2. How will you pay for the service? Does insurance cover it, or will you have to pay monthly out of pocket?

These are just a few tips about finding the right online therapist, but also make sure you have a rapport with the person. Afterall, you're spilling your guts out to them. It would be nice to have a professional relationship with someone you like and feel comfortable with, right?

When you're speaking with your therapist, be sure to mention that you're working through this book. Since you're still in the no-contact zone, ask if they think you should speak with your ex for closure and how you should go about it in a healthy way.

More on speaking with your ex is up soon!

EXERCISE 20:

PHONE-A-FRIEND.

Make sure you're ready to let go before you decide to work through this exercise. There's no coming back from it. Rachel Weinstein, MA, LCPC warns, "if you choose to do this exercise, please make sure that you choose a friend who is close to you, sensitive and has your best interests at heart."

Now it's time to pick up your phone and ask for some outside opinions about your ex. These assessments may lead you to discover some character traits you never saw in them. Ultimately it may lead you to gain the closure you need to move on.

Friend One:

1. Did I seem happy to you with my ex?

_____
_____
_____
_____

2. Did you think this relationship was good for me?

_____
_____
_____
_____

Friend Two:

1. Did I seem happy to you with my ex?

_____
_____
_____
_____

2. Did you think this relationship was good for me?

_____
_____
_____
_____

Friend Three:

1. Did I seem happy to you with my ex?

_____
_____
_____
_____

2. Did you think this relationship was good for me?

_____
_____
_____
_____

The answers your friends and family members give may hurt you, but you have to promise yourself that you will not argue or swear at or become defensive to the people that care about you most. These are opinion-based questions, which means there are no wrong answers.

Some of your friends or family members may decline to work through this exercise with you. Be prepared for that.

It would be extremely beneficial if someone who has actually met your ex could answer these questions, as the responses will allow you to gain more insight into the situation. Call as many people as you think necessary to gain a consensus.

Even if everyone absolutely loved your ex, at least you know that you can pick a good one. This will help you in the next few exercises.

EXERCISE 21:
BEGIN TO REPAIR YOUR SELF-ESTEEM.

Chances are that after a breakup of this magnitude, your confidence may be running on fumes.

After going through any type of rejection, it's normal to feel a bit shaken and not sure of your footing. The last thing we want you to do is make poor decisions when you're already feeling low (and if you're feeling low and lonely, take this time to do a guided meditation self-esteem session on YouTube and revisit the No Contact tips in this book). Keep moving forward; don't move backward!

Now, as part of your healing process, we're going to take some time to work on your self-esteem.

Lisa Bahar, licensed marriage and family therapist and licensed professional clinical counselor who specializes in Dialectical Behavior Therapy (DBT) and healthy relationship building (www.lisabahar.com) recommends these "contribute" and "comparison" activities to help boost your self-esteem.

Contribute: Instead of focusing on your feelings, devote time to something or someone that asks you to think and be present for someone other than yourself.

- Offer to walk a neighbor's dog that may be stuck in the yard or indoors all day.
- Help an elderly person tend to their unkempt garden.
- Call a friend or family and ask how they are doing. Listen to what they have to say.
- Offer to babysit for a friend or neighbor.

Compare: Use these coping skills to help with your self-esteem.

- Consider times in the past where you've had to overcome an obstacle and didn't think you would make it. Now look how far you've come and be proud of overcoming that obstacle.
- Consider the reality of someone less fortunate than you. It could be a friend or family member who is

going through a serious illness, or a homeless person, really anything that's direr than what you're going through. Now think about the reality of your situation in comparison. Does it seem as bad as it was?

There are a lot of confidence-building apps in the App store. Try one out and see what works for you.

Here are some more self-esteem boosters:

Do something you're good at. Are you a chess master? A tennis phenom? Can you solve the New York Times crossword puzzle in less than thirty minutes? No matter how mundane, it has to make you feel good to know that there's something at which you excel. Do it!

Learn something new. Whether it's cooking, dancing, or sewing, spend time learning a new skill. Adding to your repertoire of all the things that are already wonderful about you will lead to added confidence.

Volunteer your time or give money to charity if you don't want to leave your couch. There's an old saying that insists that to be happy, a person should do at least one good deed every day. Some of us might only do one good deed per year, but just know that doing something is better than doing nothing. When you do something that matters to another person, you'll feel amazing about yourself. And hopefully it'll help you realize that in this big world, you can make a difference in someone's life. And therefore, you should realize that you matter.

Acknowledge your achievements. Whether it's doing good deeds, earning awards, getting good grades, or overcoming adversity, take some time to acknowledge your achievements, no matter how big or small.

Take a few minutes and write down all of the wonderful things about yourself. Don't be afraid to brag. Go ahead and boast! Whether these are publicly celebrated qualities about you, or things that you just keep to yourself, write down what makes you special.

_____
_____
_____
_____
_____
_____
_____
_____
_____
_____
_____
_____
_____
_____

EXERCISE 22:
DISPOSE OF YOUR EX'S STUFF.

If you haven't given your ex their stuff back, it's high time to do so. If you don't think your ex wants to take charge of their belongings, then you can decide to throw them out, keep everything, or give it all to the Salvation Army/Goodwill.

If you want to keep the ex's belongings, then just put them away. Put love letters with your other (older) love letters. Tuck shirts all the way in the abyss at the back of your closet. And place romantic tokens, like teddy bears out of sight for the time being.

If you decide to give back your ex's property, make sure to text and notify that you're going to drop by and leave a bag on the porch or in front of their door. Ask your ex to do the same with your things if there's something that you really would like returned.

This might be the time that you want to speak to your ex to get closure because it's the most convenient—but it's entirely up to you. If you need to talk, then go back to your list of discussion points and see if there's something on there you need to address in order to move forward with your life. Then review the next chapter for tips about meeting/talking with your ex.

If you're going to talk, then make a game plan. What are you going to talk about? What are your boundaries (will you have sex if the opportunity presents itself?). How long will you stay? What excuse can you make to leave if you become uncomfortable? Who can you call once the meetup is over to help you assess your feelings?

More tips are available in the next chapter, so read on as you decide whether you want to meet with your ex in person, text, or even chat on the phone.

If you find yourself barreling through this book, then why not take a break? This book won't help you if you try to do it all in one day. Think about calling a friend or watching a movie.

EXERCISE 23:

MEET WITH YOUR EX

As stated in previous exercises, you absolutely do not have to perform this one if you're feeling at peace with your breakup and you're ready to stop looking back.

But if you feel you need closure, we garnered some great advice from some experts.

First things first, the biggest question you're probably asking yourself is: *How do I know if I even need closure?*

Meredith Siller, LMFT and Co-Founder at relationalassociates.com says, "We all need closure; I think the question is whether you need closure from your ex or whether it's something you want to provide to yourself. It's a misconception that we need another person to provide closure, and it's often not possible."

Jennifer Klesman, licensed therapist and author of <u>You Can't Stay There, Surviving a Breakup One Moment at a Time</u> advises, "It is important to ask yourself: 'do I just want to see them one more time?' and if you do, that is fine. But be clear with yourself if that is a major motivation or if you're searching for some answers to help you feel at peace. Look at what type of questions you have: are you asking them for answers like 'When did you stop loving me?' 'Is there someone else?' 'What did I do wrong?'

She goes on to say, "Your ex may try to protect your feelings and keep their answers vague. Be sure that what you are asking are questions that you feel that your ex will be able to answer and be mindful that they may try to protect your feelings since this can be difficult for them too."

"Also, ask yourself what are you expecting from the closure? What do you hope that it looks like? Are you hoping that the closure means your grieving is over? Are you ready to see them and maybe feel the grief all over again?"

So, you may be wondering, *What's the best way to ask for closure? How do I know they'll even respond?* Klesman says," Be honest. If you feel comfortable, admit that you're stuck on the breakup and would like to have one more conversation. Be ready for them to have their own boundaries (they may not be ready to see you in person or may not be ready to talk about it), so be flexible with what you ask of them. Say it will be just a conversation, no expectations of them, and you don't want to fight (assuming that arguing could happen)."

She also says that if you feel ready, you should meet in person at a coffee shop, or other place with a time commitment. If you meet elsewhere, she advises against consuming alcohol and suggests paying for your own beverage. To go even further, Meredith Siller recommends meeting at a new place, as opposed to a place that is sentimental for one or both of you.

If you don't want to meet in person, have your questions ready and ask them over text. Or if you're feeling really ambitious, schedule a time to talk on the phone like they used to do in olden times.

Now, if you've decided to meet in person with your ex, it's time to make a game plan. Klesman advises," Set a time frame for how long you want to meet and establish if you want any physical contact or not (like a hug) ahead of time. You don't have to share these boundaries; these can just be for you to have."

After meeting with your ex, you may be feeling a bit raw. That's normal. Klesman says you can self-soothe by seeing a friend to process the meetup, having a favorite meal, working out, journaling, or just doing whatever you want that will feel good. Siller advises, "Consider what could support each of your senses—is there a food/beverage you can have ready, a supportive movie or TV show or book, a favorite comfy outfit, a bath, an animal companion?"

Finally, Klesman says, "It is important to remember that closure comes from yourself, you already have the facts that they ended the relationship and no longer want to be with you, and beyond that, it's just details. Sometimes closure is just reopening old wounds and can be a setback, so just be careful with it."

Once again, we'd like to reiterate that you don't have to perform this exercise. Perhaps after reading the advice in this chapter, you might decide that it's not something you need—and just know that it's perfectly okay. This is all about you and your journey.

EXERCISE 24:
WRITE THE FUTURE AS IT REALLY WOULD HAVE BEEN.

What if you would have stayed with your ex? Knowing what you know now, how would your future have differed if you had stayed with your ex? Some examples are:

- My parents would never have accepted them.

- They would have continued to cheat on me.

- We would have argued constantly, and the foundation of our relationship would never have been truly solid.

- They never would have changed the demeaning way they spoke to me and therefore I would have always been trying to prove my intelligence.

- They never would have stopped beating up on me emotionally or physically and it would have scarred me more than it has already.

- I never would have been able to help or change them, because they have to decide to do that on her own. No matter the amount of effort I would have put into trying to help—they still would have to decide to change their behavior on their own. And they may never have changed.

Those are just some examples, but we wanted you to realize that there are myriad reasons that your future may not have turned out to be as peachy as you initially dreamed it would. So with that, write down the future as it really would have been:

1. _____
   _____
   _____
   _____
   _____
   _____

Write The Future As It Really Would Have Been.

2. _____

3. _____

4. _____

5. _____

6. _____
_____
_____
_____
_____
_____

7. _____
_____
_____
_____
_____
_____

8. _____
_____
_____
_____
_____
_____

9. _____
_____
_____
_____
_____
_____

EXERCISE 25:
ENVISION YOUR NEW FUTURE.

While performing research for this book, we came across a concept known as *Future Visioning*. It sounds like a new-age notion, but it's grounded in some really amazing ideas. This is probably some of the best advice you can take with you in your life, so buckle up and pay attention!

Hypnotherapist and *Future Visioning* creator Ti Caine, C.H.T. has spent 33 years helping people live life more happily and with purpose by helping them visualize and create the future they want. In regard to healing a broken heart, he says, "The only real complete healing for your breakups will be to create the future where you have the loving relationship that you really want!"

He then urges, "Think about that...Are you ever going to be really happy and satisfied with a mediocre life with no relationship at all or just with a mediocre relationship? Could you or should you be happy and satisfied with a mediocre life?"

While traditional therapy explores your past and helps you come to terms with where you are now, in *Future Visioning* the idea is that, instead of letting your past dictate your present state of being and state of mind, becoming a future-minded person will allow you to live your life with every essence of your being—mind, body and spirit—focused on a happy, fulfilling future that you create. In other words: the past doesn't create the present. The future creates the present.

But how do you visualize and create the future you want? It may take some time for you to begin to plan out what you want to happen in your future in terms of career, living situation, etc., but as you work with the future and really begin to think about it, you will discover those things in time. In fact, studies show that only 3% have a clear vision of their future, 17% have "kind of an idea" of their ideal future and 80% don't know where they're going! Guess who ends up more successful in the long run? That's right. Those 3% who have a clear vision of their future!

So, it is a good idea to design and create the future that you want, down to your career, where you want to live, etc., but for purposes of this book, let's begin the work to design and create the future that includes the type of relationship you want to be in 5 years from now. What type of relationship do you ideally want to be in 5 years from today? Think about it. In your future:

- Are you married?
- Are you in a fulfilling relationship with someone who cares about your well-being?
- Are there children?
- Where are you living?

Close your eyes and imagine your ideal future. See yourself with the love of your life. Imagine this person looking at you with love in their eyes. Imagine how they make you feel inside. Imagine the safety and security you feel just from knowing and feeling that your search for love is complete and you have truly found your soul mate and life-long partner.

Feel the warmth in your heart and feel it grow and envelop you. Feel your stress level drop. Feel your breathing deepen. Feel your hope and motivation reawaken.

Hold those feelings with you. Keep those feelings in your memory so you can call upon them at a moment's notice.

Now open your eyes. How do you feel? Relaxed? Happy? At peace? Are you a bit more hopeful about the future?

Here comes the most important part of *Future Visioning:*. Instead of thinking about the past and the things that got you to where you are now, change your focus and focus everything on your life FORWARD and be sure that every step you take in your life will lead you to that future, to that relationship, to that kind of security, to those feelings. Think about your everyday choices and how they will lead you to the future of your dreams. Live with this mindset and it will help you really think about the people you date, the way you see yourself, and the way you focus and find a renewed motivation for life and for joy.

To learn more about *Future Visioning*, visit www.ticaine.com and click on the "free materials section." There he has free meditation exercises, *Future Visioning* Worksheets, and so much more.

So, make the choice to turn your attention forward to your incredible future. Really figure out where you want your future to be and the paths you can take to get there.

EXERCISE 26:

WRITE YOUR OWN "HAPPILY EVER AFTER."

A lot of people forget to let go of the past when they are contemplating their future. But by now, you realize that you do have a future without your ex and the things you do in life actually matter in the grand scheme of things.

Plus, you have worked through self-esteem issues and have imagined a future with your dream partner. Now it's time to write your own ending. Using your journal, work on the following:

Write down what happened when you imagined your dream future. Write down how you felt. Write down where you imagined you would live. Notice every detail down to children, your job—anything you were able to imagine.

Next, write about the kind of relationship you really want to have and the qualities this person possesses. Is it someone who will finally get your jokes? Is someone who understands you and will listen to you? Is it someone who is more than willing to date you, even though you have your children every other week? What is it that you desire in your next long-term relationship?

As you write about it, start thinking more about things you want that are career and health related, or family related. Write your dream future with your dream job and your dream home and maybe even your dream car. Then in our next exercise, let's figure out how to get them.

_____
_____
_____
_____
_____
_____
_____
_____
_____
_____
_____
_____

Write Your Own "Happily Ever After."

EXERCISE 27:

CREATE PERSONAL GOALS.

Like the **Tasks List** at the beginning of the book, we want you to create bigger personal goals that will help you reach the future of your dreams. These goals do not include a relationship—these are things you can do for yourself to help build your dream future on your own, until the person of your dreams is able to join you on your journey. (And you'd best keep pursuing these goals even after you meet "the one!").

Maybe these goals involve going back to school, moving out of your apartment, starting a blog, starting a new business. Or maybe it's all of the above!

Whatever they are, just be aware of your goals, then work on small steps day-by-day (use your **Task List** if you want or write them below) to help you achieve your personal dreams. Some dreams seem too big to even imagine but tackling a little bit on a daily basis can get you closer to your goals.

Write down 5 things that you want that do not include a romantic partner or a relationship. Include a time limit to help you focus on a time to complete the goal.

Here are some ideas we came up with:

- Take a class through the Harvard Extension or EdX this year to help me in my career path, or to boost my resume.

- Join a Big Brother or Big Sister program in June.

- Go on a 5K charity walk to raise money for cancer in September.

- Hire a personal trainer by next month to come to my home and kick me out of bed every morning (or at least three days a week).

- Learn how to cook a full Thanksgiving dinner by Thanksgiving.

- Sign up for dance lessons at the local center for adult education.

- Train to run a 10K by October.

My personal goals:

1. _____
_____
_____
_____
_____

2. _____
_____
_____
_____
_____

3. _____
_____
_____
_____
_____

4. _____
_____
_____
_____
_____

Now do the research to see what you have to do to accomplish each goal. What are the steps you can take to get what you want?

First steps toward reaching my goals:

1. _____
   _____
   _____
   _____
   _____

2. _____
   _____
   _____
   _____
   _____

3. _____
   _____
   _____
   _____
   _____

Don't worry about how long it will take. This is a good start to working on the future you desire.

Refer to this checklist often. Many people complain of being "bored" after a breakup because they don't have a romantic partner around to entertain them. If you haven't completed everything on your list, then strive to finish it.

EXERCISE 28:
CHOOSE THE RIGHT PEOPLE TO DATE.

Individual sports may have different types of fouls. For example, in basketball, a technical foul occurs when a player displays unsportsmanlike non-contact behavior. The resulting punishment is losing possession of the ball, or letting the other team make free throws. A flagrant foul occurs when a player displays unsportsmanlike contact behavior (like purposely pushing another player) and is considered the most serious foul. The punishment for flagrant fouls is often immediate ejection from the game.

So, while in sports there are different kinds of fouls, in relationships, different kinds of fouls exist as well! If you find yourself experiencing a relationship rut, meaning you date the same people again and again, it's time to identify that pattern so you can make a change.

Psychotherapist Cynthia C. McKay, J.D., M.A. suggests that you make a list of relationship fouls and keep the list handy.

When you begin dating a new person, you'll refer to this list to see if there are any qualities in your new partner that reflect the Relationship Fouls on your list. We know that sometimes it can be intoxicating when you're with a new person and you can ignore a

few small faults but use this to gauge for the bigger faults—the things you promised yourself you'd stay away from.

So, let's get started with making your list.

Some people are attracted to alcoholics, some are attracted to cheaters, and some are attracted to deadbeats. Others are attracted to people who are hard to get. Some people have long-term relationships with good people, but they didn't work out for whatever reason. If you can figure out what types you're attracted to, and why you're attracted to those types of people, you can start choosing more wisely in the future. Once you figure out the code, you can use it to your advantage.

So, let's do an exercise right now to figure out the types of people you tend to date. Then you can crack the code!

Think about the last 2-3 people you have seriously dated. Write down the following traits for each one:

School level: (high school, college graduate, drop out):

Person 1: _____

Person 2: _____

Person 3: _____

Maturity level: (knew when to be serious):

Person 1: _____

Person 2: _____

Person 3: _____

Financial status: (made enough to pay their own bills, borrowed money constantly):

Person 1: _____

Person 2: _____

Person 3: _____

Parental status: (no kids, kids, kids from multiple households?):

Person 1: _____

Person 2: _____

Person 3: _____

Living situation: (lived alone, live with a roommate, or you?).

Person 1: _____

Person 2: _____

Person 3: _____

Recreational substance use: (did illegal drugs, drank responsibly?):

Person 1: _____

Person 2: _____

Person 3: _____

Legal status: (has never been arrested, has multiple DUIs, has been to jail multiple times):

Person 1: _____

Person 2: _____

Person 3: _____

Job status: (had a job, unemployed, worked 3 jobs to make ends meet):

Person 1: _____

Person 2: _____

Person 3: _____

Dependability/Reliability: (could always be counted on in times of need, was never available for you, turned off the cell phone on nights out with friends, wouldn't answer phone calls):

Person 1: _____

Person 2: _____

Person 3: _____

Are you seeing any kind of patterns here? Consider these traits in each new person you date. What are the traits you definitely want to stay away from?

Now create a 2 column "tolerability list". On the left, put down things that you didn't love about these guys or girls, but could tolerate in the future. On the right, put down things that you absolutely will not stand for in a new relationship.

Tolerability list:

Things I didn't love:	Things I can tolerate:
_____	_____
_____	_____
_____	_____
_____	_____
_____	_____
_____	_____
_____	_____
_____	_____

While you're in this mindset, what are some other patterns you can determine from previous relationships—those flagrant fouls that will cause you to immediately dismiss someone?

Now, when you begin dating someone, refer to your list of fouls. It will help to have it written down, so definitely take the time to work on this exercise. Add to your list as needed!

Be smart when dating and use this exercise to help you find a healthy relationship. It may take some time to recognize a healthy relationship and find it, but don't worry about that. Just think long-term

EXERCISE 29:
MAKE A DATING GAME PLAN

Some of the people reading this book will not need a dating game plan. Some of you are so seasoned that you'll be able to pick up, move on and date someone else as soon as you've put down this book (or maybe you're already seeing someone and just wanted to finish!). But some of you may have been in very long-term relationships (including marriage) and may not be prepared for dating in this day and age. Don't worry. We brought in an expert to help you plan for this stage in the game (when you're ready, of course!).

Dr. LeslieBeth Wish is a nationally honored psychologist & licensed clinical social worker, and author of Smart Relationships. To buy her book, learn more about her (and receive a gift!), go to her website www.lovevictory.com. We asked her a few questions about dating again. First, we asked her how long someone should wait before dating after a long-term relationship. Her answer?

"The quick answer is 'not immediately.'" She says, "Before you get back out there, be sure you can answer these questions about your most recent relationship:"

- Why did I choose this person?
- What was going on in my life at that time?
- Did I like who I became in this relationship?
- How did I contribute to the problems/unhappiness?
- What am I learning about me?

We would also add that you must understand why you're dating. Are you looking for a hookup? Or a long-term relationship? Maybe you're lonely and just need a friend? These are good things to determine before you get back out there. These are also nice things to share on dating profiles and such. If you're not looking for a long-term relationship, then please, put that on your profile. It isn't fair to the person you're dating (if they ARE looking for a long-term relationship) to waste their time.

On how and where to go about meeting new people, Dr. Wish offered the following advice: "Social media sites are only as successful as your profile and your willingness to connect with people. You usually don't feel 'chemistry' [through a screen]. That feeling, after all, has drawn you into relationships that didn't work!"

"In your profile, don't list all your likes in music, television shows, and long walks on the beach. List your positive personality qualities— 'kind & reliable,' for example—and ask for the same in the other people!"

Here are some dating websites and apps to check out:

- Match (for men, women, gay & straight of all ages, for dating)
- eHarmony (for people of any age, searching for a soulmate)
- Christian Mingle (for Christians looking for other Christians)
- JDate (for Jewish people seeking other Jewish people)
- OKCupid (for all ages & sexual preferences)
- OurTime (for people 50+)
- Hinge (built on an acclaimed Nobel-Prize winning algorithm that is supposed to help you find the right person)
- Grindr (the #1 free dating app for the LGBTQ+ community)
- Tinder (for all ages & sexual preferences)

On meeting people from online in person, Dr. Wish stresses, "Be smart—and override those tendencies to be 'too nice and accepting.' You don't want to end up as the next feature story on *Dateline*. Don't give out your address. Tell your friends where you are going on this date."

More advice: Keep your cell phone on. Share your location with friends/family. Don't go on dates far away from where you live. The last place you want to be is in his or her car on a long romantic ride far away from taxis or your home. And don't think you can outsmart your brain: Don't tempt sex way too soon by going back to one of your places. If you like each other, find a hotel lobby or bar. They tend to stay open late."

On attempting to meet people in person, Dr. Wish suggests these two exercises:

"Make a 'personal promise pact' that you will go out twice [or once] a week to an event that interests you. But you are not allowed to leave until you've introduced yourself—and spend time talking—to people. They could even be someone you just want to befriend. You can say: "Hi, I'm___, what's your name?" As you go through your daily errands at the post office or grocery store, start a similar conversation. However, you can begin it by just turning to that person in line or in front of the crackers and say: Have you tried these?"

And about being ready for sex, Dr. Wish says, "Take your time—especially if you have children. You don't want your kids to think you are running a parade of new people! You are ready for sex when you know most (preferably all) of these things:

- You've known this person through some good and not so good times. People's emotions and choices of partners change during life's ups and downs.
- You've been together with each other's friends, so you know how this person interacts.
- You like and respect who you are in this relationship—and you feel the same about this new person.
- You share common life values and goals.
- This new person makes you feel warm (loved and accepted and celebrated) and safe (you can rely on this person to be there for the good and bad)
- You laugh together.
- You feel "known" and understood—and you "get" the other person
- You enjoy being together—especially just hanging out. It's "easy" to be together.

Some people are fine with just hooking up, and that's okay. But if you're really looking for something, perhaps consider Dr. Wish's advice.

What about those of us with children?

On being ready to introduce your children to a new love interest, Dr. Wish advises, "For starters, think twice about having your kids meet EVERY new person. School age children and teens can get anxious quickly. They wonder: *Is this someone I should worry about and get to know?* Think through their eyes."

She goes on to explain, "Some people recommend that you introduce a new person of interest right away. The idea is that you can see how the kids and this new person interact. It's not a bad idea. It can ease your new love and the children into getting used to each other. But it may not give you all the key information you need. In the beginning, when the emotional stakes are not as high, it is easier for your new person and children to be on "best behavior"—or to just sort of be disinterestedly polite. It's usually when your new person and the children know or sense that this new person is very important that signs of difficulty occur. You can use both approaches."

The bottom line, "If the relationship becomes special, talk about your views on who disciplines the children and what you expect from each other."

Finally, Dr. Wish offers this advice, "Know yourself! Do not go on dates with the idea of finding THE

ONE/YOUR SOUL MATE. One of the main reasons that people are afraid to date again is that they have lost trust in their love judgment/intuition. Instead, change the goal of dating to learning to read people accurately. Go on that second or third date to test your intuition—and to give second chances. The best dates are "un-dates" where you hang out together.

We couldn't agree more. Choose dating to get to know people, and more importantly, get to know yourself and understand what you like, what turns you on (emotionally and intellectually and physically) and take the time to hone your dating skills. You don't have to marry the first person you go out with.

As a rule, be nice. You'll never go wrong if your main goal is to treat the people you date with respect and kindness.

EXERCISE 30:

GET OUT OF THE HOUSE IF YOU HAVEN'T YET!

It's time. You have done all this work. You may not be ready to move on to someone else just yet, but you can get out of the house and see what it's like outside again. Some fresh air might do you good.

Whether it's going out on the town with your friends, volunteering, or just going for a walk, here are some ideas to help inspire you to get off your couch and move forward with your life.

- Book a plane ticket for an exotic destination (with or without your friends) if you can afford it.
- Visit your favorite animal shelter and adopt that pet you've always wanted.

- Drive to Vegas with your best friend and don't go to sleep for two days.

- Go to church for services or take part in a church event.

- Invite your parents to lunch.

- Try to get your friends together and hit the town. See a play, go to the bar, go dancing - even rent a limo! The world is your oyster.

In short, do whatever makes you feel comfortable within your particular lifestyle, and start living your life for yourself, not for your ex.

FINAL THOUGHTS.

We hope that after analyzing the rise and fall of your relationship, you have come to the realization that:

- Your relationship had both good and bad qualities.
- It ended because it was time for it to end.
- Neither your ex nor you were a perfect member in the relationship.
- The relationship is truly over.

We hope that when you are ready to meet someone, you will be as open and as trusting as you can possibly be. We hope that when you are ready, you will meet someone great.

Please feel free to go to our private group www.facebook.com/groups/breakupworkbook3/ to discuss any problems you may still have in relation to your ex, to yourself, or to your health. It's important to surround yourself with people who care and sometimes your friends can grow tired of hearing the same story. You'll find that nobody is more helpful than a person who understands exactly what you are going through.

Before you go out in the world ready to date, we wanted to share with you some commonsense advice:

Get used to heartbreak. Every relationship you ever have will fail until you meet the person you marry. Even after you get married, that relationship is not guaranteed to last forever. Invest in a nice fuzzy blanket, comfortable pajamas, Netflix, and self-help books, for such occasions that you may need them.

Remember that dating is supposed to be fun! It's not a job and you don't have to marry someone just because you went on one date. Have fun.

Take care when choosing a new person to date. Remember that it's a choice.

Don't just jump into a relationship with the first person who shows interest. Make sure the person will add goodness to your life.

If someone breaks up with you, remember that there's nothing wrong with you. You just weren't right for that person. Or any of the other people you've dated. Repeat: there's nothing wrong with you. It happens to everybody.

Remember that some people only view sex as an extra-curricular activity. If you really want to be in a lasting relationship, think carefully about when it's appropriate to sleep with your new love interest.

Remember that some people really don't care if you're smart/accomplished/interesting/funny. Some people really only like you for your hot body. Use what you've learned in this book to discern their intentions.

Break old patterns. If you meet a person who doesn't meet your standards, recognize those relationship fouls. Don't allow yourself to keep dating the same type of person over and over again.

Remember how incredible you are. If you meet a person who lies to you and cheats on you, don't ever put the blame on yourself. You don't deserve to be treated poorly. If the person sucks, then walk away.

You are smart. You are worth it. You are powerful. Believe it.

RESOURCES.

If you're in immediate danger of overdosing or have harmed yourself, or are ready to do so, call 911 or an emergency provider right away.

Please read the following and seek medical attention if you are feeling suicidal, or the breakup is interfering with your everyday life — taking care of your children, getting to work on time, etc.

If you are feeling as if you want to hurt yourself or others, please seek help.

If you're feeling suicidal, now is not the time to be proud. Just be honest and ask for help, or just go to your local hospital.

Here are some of the ways that you can get the help you need:

Call a help hotline (long distance charges may apply):

Outside of the United States:

Visit this website to see suicide hotline numbers for over 62 countries

http://www.suicide.org/international-suicide-hotlines.html

In the United States:

US National Suicide Prevention Hotline:

1. 800.SUICIDE

US National Suicide Prevention Lifeline:

1.800. 273.TALK

US Depression Hotline:

1.630. 482.9696

Alcoholism and Drug addiction hotline -

1.888. 268.9124

If you're in immediate danger of overdosing or have harmed yourself, or are ready to do so, call 911 or an emergency provider right away.

For suicide:

http://www.suicide.com

www.suicide.org

http://www.nami.org

For depression:

www.depression.org

http://www.stressgroup.com/depression

DepressionAndAnxietyRecovery.com

For domestic violence:

http://www.ndvh.org

For alcoholism:

Alcoholics Anonymous - www.aa.org

For families or friends of alcoholics:

https://al-anon.org/

http://www.al-anon.alateen.org/

For drug addiction and families and friends of drug addicts:

www.ProjectKnow.com

BREAKUP QUOTES:

In addition to our commonsense breakup advice, we collected these stories and quotes that we thought you'd appreciate!

"Time heals all wounds. If you don't feel better in a month, you can always burn your ex's house down."

~ Jenny Lawson, author of Let's Pretend This Never Happened (A Mostly True Memoir)

https://www.thebloggess.com

"You need to realize that we all want so desperately to connect with one other. We want to connect with something that is real, and when we do, it is like our spirit jumps and feels so ALIVE! When that goes away, the love hangover is very intense. You may never find love again, I may never find love again, but there is love and we both had it at one point in our lives. It was amazing! Some people may never find that kind of love, so be happy that you did, because it was real, and it was true! Now chin up! You never know when love may find you again; I met my love at a BBQ!"

~ Justin Tranchita, singer songwriter

"After dating a gal for four years and proposing she broke up with me for another guy. I was heartbroken and absolutely devastated. My grandmother gave me this advice- 'Hon, I know it hurts, but you gotta let it go.' Those simple words helped me as easy at is sounds it isn't, but I found the more I let go and didn't think or dwell on it the better I felt."

~Doug Briney, Independent Country Music Association Award Winner
and Nashville Universe Award Nominee

dougbriney.com

"I guess the best advice I could give is that time will heal everything. It may not feel like it right away . . . or even a while after, but one day you will wake up, and you will be over it. Also, never settle for anything less then you deserve. Sometimes people walk out of our lives to leave room for something better to walk in!"

~Alyssa Morrissey, Wire Award-winning country artist

alyssamorrissey.com

"Best breakup advice I can give: Pulling yourself out of a pit of despair and soggy Kleenex is not the easiest thing to do, but rest assured, there is a light at the end of the tunnel. Why settle for Mr. or Ms. Right "Now" when Mr. or Ms. "Right" is still out there waiting for you... Let go and move on because change is a good thing..."

~Amy Rose, International Music and Entertainment Association Country Entertainer of the Year, Independent Country Music Association Award Winner, Nashville Universe Award Winner

www.amyrosemusic.com

Best breakup advice I can give: "Sleep it off, tomorrow will bring a new day and a better chance at being with all of the other women who are still out there."

~Jiggley Jones, Award-winning singer/songwriter

www.jiggleyjones.com

"The best thing that I would say is either if you've just broken up with someone, or you've been broken up with, is to focus on your physical health. To work out, maybe get that 'revenge body'. If you're working out and you're living a healthy, physical lifestyle, that's what you need to do because going through a breakup is not easy—so channel that into something positive.

~Jason Zone Fisher – Host of Coaster Quest on the Travel Channel

---

www.ingramcontent.com/pod-product-compliance
Lightning Source LLC
Chambersburg PA
CBHW051559010526
44118CB00023B/2756